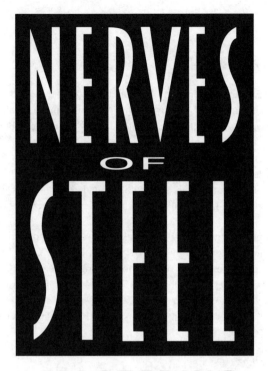

NERVES OF STEEL

MASTERING YOUR EMOTIONS TO BEAT THE MARKET

CLIFFORD PISTOLESE

PROBUS PUBLISHING COMPANY
Chicago, Illinois
Cambridge, England

ISBN 1-55738-467-3

Printed in the United States of America

BC

1   2   3   4   5   6   7   8   9   0

I dedicate this book to my father, Anthony F. Pistolese. You had the courage to make an initial investment in the stock market in the depths of the Great Depression. With nerves of steel you made additional purchases when selling panics drove prices down in the years that followed. Your outstanding fortitude and patience have been a life-long inspiration to me.

Table of Contents

Contents

Contents

Contents

List of Figures and Tables

Preface

Some investors experience a variety of emotions in the stock market. A vision of great wealth—easily obtainable—fuels their greed. Their initial reaction to a sizeable paper profit is to feel proud and boast about their achievement. They revel in bull market rallies and fall in love with a stock that multiplies in price. They are caught up in the euphoria as the market approaches a top and speculate with funds they can't afford to lose.

They become stubborn and disbelieving when their stocks begin to fall. They worry and become fearful as a bear market erodes their confidence. After holding on as long as their fortitude allows, they surrender to mass panic and sell out in despair after listening to those who predict doom at the bottom of a market cycle.

◆ ◆ ◆

Since its inception, the stock market has provided both opportunity for the prudent, informed person and danger for the unwary, inpulsive individual. The former type of investor makes a rational decision after considering both the reward and the risk. The latter makes an emotional decision based on hunches, rumors or hot tips.

This book will help you understand how emotional decision making may be hurting your chances for success. It outlines long-term strategies to help you avoid the emotional stress of sharp, short-term price fluctuations. It provides suggestions for controlling your emotional reactions to stock market events. And it will help you get started on the road toward achieving your financial goals.

The first three chapters describe the general problems associated with emotional investing and contain an exercise to assess your susceptibility. The last seven chapters provide strategies, tactics and suggestions for controlling your emotions rather than letting them control you. Here's a chapter-by-chapter overview of the contents.

Chapter 1 details the losses of money and time which can occur when investors make buying decisions based on greed while ignoring high risk.

Chapter 2 analyzes the emotions generated in the market and describes the negative impact they have on decision making.

Chapter 3 provides a self-analysis exercise which measures your emotional susceptibility to events in the market and to price changes in your stocks.

Chapter 4 describes the causes of emotional decisions in the market. It asks questions to help you analyze your vulnerability to those causal factors. And it presents a framework and suggestions for developing control over your emotions.

Chapter 5 outlines long-term strategies to help you avoid emotional reactions to short-term market conditions and price changes. It also outlines the characteristics, advantages and disadvantages of each strategy to help you decide which one is most appropriate for you.

Chapter 6 delineates the stock chart patterns which characterize market tops and bottoms.

Chapter 7 presents guidelines for selling near the top of a market cycle.

Chapter 8 provides a review of market panics of the past and gives suggestions for dealing with panics in the future.

Chapters 9 and 10 outline how to develop a comfortable, profitable long-term relationship with a competent broker. They also provide suggestions for avoiding the types of customer/broker relationships which can do more harm than good.

Chapter 1

 # Hazards of Emotional Decisions

Riding the Roller Coaster

The stock market is well known for episodes of mass emotions. At times, euphoric buying propels the market upward like a rocket. On less happy occasions, panic selling causes it to fall like a boulder crashing down a mountain. In either of these situations, many people make emotional decisions and later, after the supercharged atmosphere has calmed down, come to regret their actions.

In 1929 speculation, greed and euphoria pushed stock prices to record heights. But a panic sell-off began in October of that year, and prices fell precipitously. During the years of the depressed economy that followed, fear of still lower stock prices induced many to sell and suffer large financial losses.

In the mid-thirties an economic recovery resulted in persistent buying on the stock market. But in 1937 waves of emotional selling sent the market down quickly. Many investors panicked, sold out, and took heavy losses.

The market recovered as domestic manufacturers were called upon to produce the massive amounts of military hardware, and other goods necessary to win World War II. Afterward, in 1946 when manufacturers lost their production orders from the government and available credit contracted quickly, the market declined sharply. The market rose again through the late forties and the fifties. But the rise was accompanied by accelerating inflation, and when the Federal Reserve Board raised interest rates in 1962, the economy contracted and the market took a short, but steep plunge as many investors sold in panic.

In late 1972 a buying euphoria came to an end, and the market declined in 1973 as investors' fears grew. In 1974 the Arabs initiated their first oil embargo of the western industrialized nations. Taken by surprise, many investors visualized an economic disaster caused by the oil shortage and sold out in desperation.

In the mid-eighties the market rose to record highs. But on October 19, 1987 the market plunged in the greatest one-day selling panic ever. Some people who had made fortunes during the long previous rise could not stand the stress and sold out at great losses near the bottom of the decline. But others, who controlled their emotions, were able to recoup their paper losses when the market subsequently recovered.

Did you experience any of these rides on the emotional roller coaster of the stock market? Did the mass hysteria of other investors and speculators affect you? Did you participate in euphoric buying or panic selling and regret it later? Or were you one of the few who were able to control their reactions and avoid the hazards of emotional decisions made under high-stress conditions?

This book will help you to analyze your emotional reactions and susceptibilities in the market. It suggests methods for establishing control over your emotions instead of letting them control you. And it presents long-term strategies for dealing with the short- and intermediate-term market fluctuations which can confuse and mislead you.

The Emotional Gamut

To appreciate the nature of the emotions that can interfere with your judgment, let's review how they might arise if your stock took a ride on a roller coaster (see Figure 1–1).

Greed: The Motivation

Your motivation for buying a stock may be a combination of greed and the hope that the value of the investment will grow. If the price starts rising, you will be pleased at having made a good selection.

Figure 1–1   A Ride on a Roller Coaster

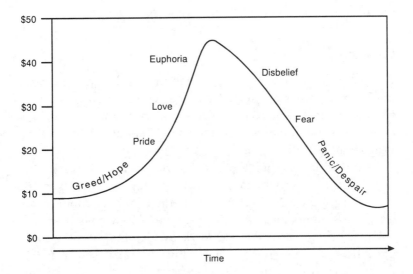

Feeling Pride

As your paper profit increases, you might become eager to tell friends and associates about the stock. You might make statements like, "Last month I bought some ABC company at ten dollars a share. It's already up to fifteen. I'm betting it'll go even higher." By stating your opinion regarding the future action of the stock, your ego becomes involved with the price performance.

A Kind of Love

When the price rises above twenty dollars a share, you are happy your prediction was correct. As it moves even higher, you may become emotionally attached to the stock. In an odd sense you may fall in love with a stock which performs well. If you hear someone express an opinion that the stock is overpriced at this level, you might be offended. You might rise to its defense as though someone you love were under attack.

Euphoric Joy

When the price rises to thirty, your money has tripled. You might very well want to tell anyone who'll listen about this wonderful stock. You could become convinced the price will go higher. (There's nothing but good news about this company. Why shouldn't it go higher?)

And it does. When the price moves up toward forty, you might become euphoric. Making money beyond your expectations can produce a joyful feeling. Is the company about to release some good news? What could it be? A few days later you see an article in *The Wall Street Journal* which indicates the company held a press conference for financial analysts. In it the Chief Executive Officer (CEO) predicted that earnings for the coming quarter would be higher and further predicted that earnings for the year would set an all-time record. He also said the next few years would witness continuing strong earnings growth because of favorable market conditions.

How wonderful! All you have to do is hold on to see the price rise further. By projecting the current rate of price increase, you might convince yourself the price could reach one hundred dollars a share. After all, the CEO is certainly the best source of reliable information about the company.

Signs of Trouble

The following day you check the price to see how high it has gone. To your surprise it has only risen twenty-five cents a share—hitting a peak of $45.00. You had expected it to rise at least a few dollars. Well, you can afford to be patient. You're in for the long haul. But still you wonder why the price didn't go up more.

Over the next few days the price fluctuates between forty-four and forty-five dollars a share. You hope it is just taking a breather. It has more than quadrupled since you bought it, and you feel it is just a matter of time before the price resumes its upward movement. But then the price drops back into the low forties. You are surprised by that move in view of the positive outlook in the *Journal* article.

The first element of doubt surfaces. For a brief time you think about selling, but decide not to unless you can receive the top price of $45.00. You become nervous about the situation because this is the first sizable decline since your purchase.

Disbelief and Denial

Several weeks pass, and you are surprised to see the price decline below forty. With the terrific prospects for the company, how could the price could drop so much? Could it be a temporary aberration? Maybe some insiders are trying to drive the price down so they can pick up more shares. Perhaps they've spread unfavorable rumors. You haven't seen anything in the financial papers or magazines about the company recently. You call your broker to ask if there's any news. The broker hasn't heard any. You are in a quandary. What happened? The price shouldn't be this low, should it? You struggle to convince yourself that others will recognize this and drive the price back up. There is no bad news—not even a rumor. You wait for the price to resume its climb. But it doesn't. Instead it starts to trade in the low thirties. Why should the price decline? It just doesn't make sense. You call your broker again and ask him to call you immediately if he hears any news on the company.

Fear Rears Its Head

In the next months the price drifts below thirty. You become fearful and call your broker every day. When the next quarterly earnings report is published it shows a rise, but only by five cents a share. Everyone had expected much more.

Soon, the price declines into the mid-twenties. Should you sell? You still have a good profit. You struggle to control your growing fear by assuming the next earnings report will be much better. You would feel foolish if you sell and the price starts moving up again. You try to reassure yourself the price won't go below twenty, and decide to hold on.

Your sense of foreboding increases. Each time you check the price in the paper, you're afraid it will be lower. And it usually is. The persistent erosion of your once huge profit makes you feel betrayed. You become too embarrassed to talk about the stock with your friends. But perhaps the stock can make a comeback and prove you right. One of your friends advises you to sell and take your profit, but you ignore her advice and hold on. The next quarterly earnings report is late. What could be causing the delay? Your broker doesn't know.

A few days later the *Journal* gives the dismaying explanation: several officers of the company have been fired for falsifying sales figures and other financial data. A whistle blower in the accounting department contacted the Securities Exchange Commission which ordered an audit of the company's books. The CEO has resigned and cannot be reached for comment.

A knot develops in the pit of your stomach. The following morning your anxiety increases when your broker says the opening in the stock has been delayed because of excess sell orders. After three hours of agonizing uncertainty, the stock begins trading in the low teens. Almost all your profits are gone! How could this happen?

The price holds above ten dollars for a while. If all the bad news is out, maybe the price will recover. But there is more bad news in the *Journal* a few days later. Corporate officers have been heavy sellers of the stock in the last few months. This news scares other stockholders also. Some of them sell to cut their losses. The price slides below ten in the following weeks.

You are in constant fear of seeing your investment decline further. The price drops to seven. How low can it go? One day your broker calls to tell you about the rumor he heard: the company may be forced to file for protection under Chapter 11 of the bankruptcy code.

Panic Takes Over

You are overwhelmed by a wave of despair. The more you think about the situation, the more panicky you become. Finally, you can bear no more. You tell the broker to sell at the market price. The sale will be made at six dollars a share. How very unfortunate!

Can You Maintain Control?

Some people who buy stocks are not prepared to deal with the emotions that arise during roller coaster rides like the one described above. They let their feelings take control. If you have never experienced such a ride on a roller coaster stock, you may believe you would not feel those emotions . . . and you might not. However, until you find yourself on a roller coaster stock, you should not assume that you would be immune to those feelings.

The downward slide of a roller coaster ride can take the price back to where it began, somewhat higher, or lower. In the worst case, the price declines until the stock becomes worthless. If you decide to become a long-term investor, you should be aware that roller coaster rides have happened to many stocks in the past and can happen to many more in the future.

Since no two individuals are identical, and emotional reactions vary from person to person, the preceding chart is not strictly representative. For some people, greed and hope are more pervasive than shown and can coexist with pride, love, euphoria, or disbelief until fear or panic take over. Some people may be too sensible to fall in love with a stock or to become euphoric. Some stay in a declining stock because of a combination of stubborn pride and disbelief. Others may experience fear, but not surrender to panic. The fears of some will be so disturbing they won't sleep well at night. Some may never become fearful or panicky, but just decide to salvage something and sell sometime during the long decline.

Roller Coaster Stocks

Below are a few of the many companies whose stocks took their investors on roller coaster rides.

Western Union

This company provided telegraphic and other communications services for many years. In 1974 its stock sold for $8.00 a share. As its earnings increased, the share price climbed to $54.00 in 1982. But competition from other communication companies gradually eroded the company's market share and profits. Its stock price fell under 25¢ per share in 1991. The once proud name of Western Union can no longer be found in the stock listings because the company changed its name to New Valley Corporation. (Western Union now offers its services as a subsidiary of the New Valley Corporation.)

Bank of New England

The stock of this major regional bank with 444 offices in New England states traded below $10.00 per share in 1977. Based on a trend of increasing earnings, the share price reached $39.00 in 1986. A decline in the economy of New England, and a slump in the real estate market decimated the bank's earnings and assets. The price of its stock fell to a few pennies a share by 1990. Federal regulators declared the bank insolvent and took it over in January, 1991.

Wang Laboratories

The common stock of this computer company was the darling of speculators during the last half of 1982 and the first half of 1983. Based on high profit margins and a strong up trend in earnings, its shares went from $12.00 to $42.50 in that time period. Subsequently, the fortunes of the company took a turn for the worse when it failed to make the switch into personal computers and lost market share to the major domestic and foreign competitors. Additional problems for the company developed when two Japanese competitors infringed on Wang's patent of single-inline-memory-modules for IBM computers. High interest charges added to Wang's woes, and the company suspended dividend payments in 1989. In 1992 the stock price went below $2.00 per share, and the company declared bankruptcy in August of that year.

Unisys Corporation

This is one of the largest manufacturers of computers and related equipment. Unisys shares rose from $9.00 in 1982 to $48.00 in 1987 as its earnings increased. But intense competition within the computer industry reduced its market share. And high interest charges on borrowed capital resulted in large losses in 1989 and 1990. The stock price fell to $1.75 in early 1991.

Pan American World Airways

This airline pioneered commercial airline services and international air travel. In the early part of 1985 Pam Am common stock was selling for $4.00 per share. As the prospects for earnings improved, the price rose to $9.25 in 1986. But the continuing increase in competition due to the deregulation of the airlines, and the sudden decrease of international air travel because of the Persian Gulf war combined to force the company into bankruptcy. In late 1991 the company filed for bankruptcy. The last assets of Pan Am were sold at auction in August of 1992. The proceeds went to the bond holders. The stock holders received nothing.

LTV Corporation

The share price of this conglomerate went from $5.00 in 1978 to a high of $26.125 in 1981 based on good earnings from its aerospace and defense industry segments. However, losses due to slowdowns in its oil field equipment, electronic, and steel segments in the early and mid 1980s created severe cash flow problems. The company fell behind by more than three billion dollars in payments to its employee pension funds. Because of this overwhelming liability and continuing operational losses, the company declared bankruptcy in 1986. The share price dropped to less than $1.00 in 1991.

Lionel Corporation

For many years Lionel has been one of the best-known companies in the toy manufacturing industry. The price of its shares rose from $1.00 in the 1970s to a high of $13.875 in 1981. With the increasing competition from other toy companies in the 1980s, its market share declined, and it was unable to maintain its previous profitability. In 1985 it ended dividend payments. The price of its shares dropped to $.375 in 1992.

Carter Hawley Hale

This company owns and operates several chains of department stores in California and some other western and sunbelt states. The share price rose from $22.00 in 1985 to $77.00 in 1987. To avoid a takeover by The Limited chain, the company assumed more than a billion dollars of debt. When consumer spending declined in subsequent years, the company was unable to meet the interest charges on this debt and filed for bankruptcy in February, 1991. Its share price hit a low of $1.00 later that year.

Russ Togs

This company makes and sells apparel for men, women, and children. The share price in 1982 was $5.50 and rose to $24.125 in 1988. Sales, market share, and earnings declined for the next few years, and the company suffered losses in 1990 and 1991.

The dividend was omitted in December 1990. The share price dropped to a low of $2.25 in late 1991.

Harcourt Brace Jovanovich

This company is a large publisher of textbooks and other books. The share price was $4.25 in 1982. Its business prospered for the next few years, and the share price peaked at $63.75 in 1987. After assuming 1.8 billion dollars in debt, the company was unable to maintain its earnings and experienced large losses starting in 1987. Dividends were discontinued in 1988. The price of the stock declined to a low of $.375 in mid-1991.

Table 1–1 shows the price swings of some additional stocks that have taken roller coaster rides.

Figure 1–1 illustrated how a sharp rise in price followed by a deep decline can elicit a broad range of emotions. Other types of price movements also draw out strong emotions. The following sections present these additional price patterns and describe their potential emotional characteristics and financial consequences.

Buying at the Top

What are the conditions under which you, or anyone else, might buy at the top? Perhaps you are one of those who normally has little interest in the stock market. Earning a living, raising a family, socializing with friends, and pursuing your hobby take up most of your time and attention. Following the ups and downs of the market may not be particularly interesting to you. Economics may not have been your favorite subject in school.

You earn a good salary, pay your bills, and place your savings in a money market fund, a certificate of deposit, or some other relatively safe investment. Perhaps you're saving for a

Table 1-1   More Roller Coaster Rides

Company Name	Early Price & Year	Intervening High Price & Year	Later Price & Year
Allied Products	$5.50 '77	$45.50 '86	$1.87 92
American Shipbuilding	1.76 '75	17.00 '81	1.13 '91
Baltimore Bancorp	8.50 '85	24.50 '86	3.75 '90
Bank of Boston	11.00 '84	37.00 '87	3.00 '91
Bolt Beranek	9.00 '84	30.00 '87	4.00 '90
Borden Chemical	10.00 '87	24.00 '89	7.50 '90
Caesars World	15.00 '87	44.00 '89	10.13 '90
Commodore International	11.00 '81	60.00 '83	4.50 '90
Continental Airlines	3.00 '74	51.50 '87	.12 '91
Data General	14.00 '82	75.00 '85	3.50 '90
Eatle-Picher	20.00 '85	53.00 '87	.87 '92
Glen Federal	11.00 '85	33.00 '87	3.50 '90
Goodyear Tire	30.00 '86	75.00 '87	12.88 '90
Hilton Hotels	51.00 '89	116.00 '89	26.38 '90
Mellon Bank	35.00 '84	72.00 '86	17.68 '90
Monarch Capital	20.00 '85	90.00 '87	.38 '90
National Education	8.00 '85	30.00 '88	1.87 '91
Teradyne	7.00 '82	39.00 '84	3.75 '90

Note: The entries in this list were selected from the New York and American Stock Exchanges. Hundreds of additional roller coaster rides have occurred on those exchanges and in the over-the-counter markets.

down payment on your own home or another major purchase. This nest egg could be growing steadily and maybe you'll have enough to buy what you want in a few more years. When friends have given you tips on the market, you've been able to resist the temptation to risk your hard earned cash.

However, at some point, skyrocketing stock prices might push the market into the newspapers' headlines. Magazine articles may then relate stories about stocks which have gained fifty percent or more within a few months. Your friends and business associates may discuss the companies they own and boast about their large paper profits. If so, it could seem that everyone else is making large capital gains, while your investment is only returning a small amount of interest.

After a few months of feeling left out, you might want to play the market yourself. You still have a long way to go before you reach your savings goal. Why not buy a stock and take a short cut to get the cash you need? Perhaps you could have it in a few months instead of a few years. The thought is very enticing. The next time a friend gives you a hot tip, you listen with great interest. It's about a small company that's researching a cure for the Acquired Immune Deficiency Syndrome (AIDS). This friend says she knows one of the officers in the company who claims they're on the verge of a breakthrough. Your friend says she has already doubled her money in the stock and expects it to skyrocket within a week as the news leaks out.

On the basis of this story, you might decide there is no time to waste and place an order to buy at the market. However, when the confirmation slip arrives in the mail a few days later, the price of the stock has peaked and is heading lower. That's just the beginning of the bad news. The rest of the painful story is shown in Figure 1–2, Buying at the Top.

Of course this is a case of extremely bad timing, but there are quite a few people who only become interested in the market when it is front page news. They feel they are missing the boat as they focus their attention on the big profits they believe

Figure 1–2   Buying at the Top

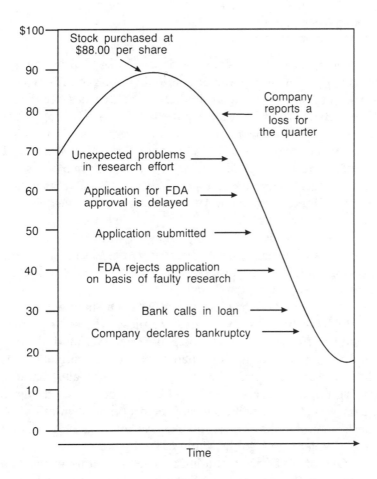

others are making. When the market is approaching or at its peak, their unleashed greed can induce them to make an untimely purchase of a popular, but overpriced, stock.

Fishing for the Bottom

Are you attracted by bargains? Who isn't? The thought of finding an apparent bargain can be an exciting prospect. The type of stock that attracts a bargain hunter is one that has declined a long distance from its peak. Figure 1–3, Bottom Fishing, illustrates such a downward movement in price. The record high price of the stock was $96.00 per share. Since then it declined over 50 percent to $40.00 per share. When the price of a stock declines such a large percentage, it can look like a bargain. In a situation like this you might very well ask yourself the question, "Could this be the bottom?"

The answer is that nobody knows. All too often a person who buys a stock primarily because it has declined a large amount is likely to be disappointed. (See Figure 1–4 to see the potential result of bottom fishing.)

If you had bought this stock at $40.00 a share, your error would have been that you tried to guess where the bottom might be. Instead, one should be patient and wait until the bottom has time to form. (Information on bottom formations as displayed in stock price charts is presented in a later chapter.) Trying to guess where a stock will bottom out is like trying to guess when a ball will bounce after dropping it into a pitch black hole of unknown depth. You can only know it has hit bottom when you hear the sound of the impact.

One of the most frustrating and self-defeating games you can play in the market is presuming you know where a stock price will reach bottom. Another factor to consider before you go bottom fishing or bargain hunting is that some companies

Figure 1-3   Bottom Fishing

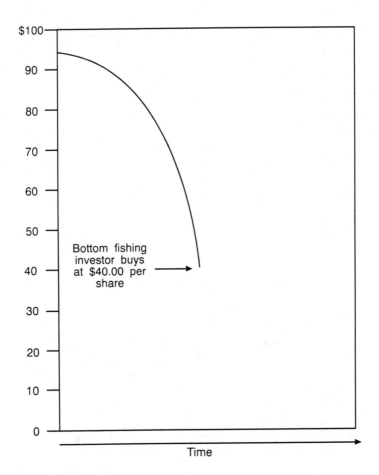

Figure 1–4   Potential Result of Bottom Fishing

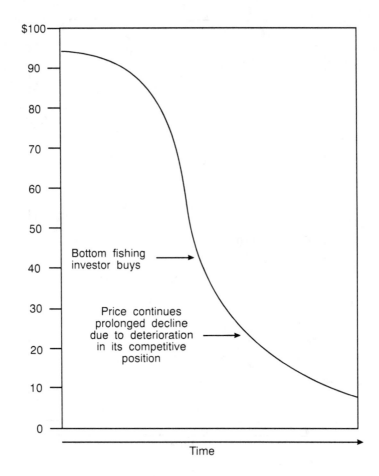

never recover from a loss of competitiveness. As their share of the market contracts, their profits decline or turn into losses. Some of these companies are forced to declare bankruptcy and/or go out of business—and their stocks may become worthless.

Bottom Fishing Is Hazardous

The temptation to fish for the bottom prematurely is a strong one. The primary motivation is excessive greed based on the idea of making a quick profit when the price of the stock rebounds sharply. But if a company's basic competitive position has changed for the worse, the decline may go much further. Below are some examples of companies whose stock prices declined by huge percentages after they started into their downward spiral.

American Savings Bank

In early 1986 the stock of this large savings bank in New York state sold at a high of $25.50. In subsequent years the weak commercial real estate market in the region led to substantial losses. In late 1989 a bottom fisher could have bought the stock for less than $10.00 a share. A year and a half later the stock traded at prices below one dollar. In the middle months of 1991 it dipped to a low of sixty-two-and-a-half cents per share. At that price, it had declined more than 97 percent from its peak value.

Circle K

The shares of this large operator of convenience stores were trading as high as $18.625 in mid-1987. As a result of expanding too rapidly, it was unable to service its large debt and also couldn't counter the intense competition in the convenience store industry. It filed for protection under the Bankruptcy Code in May, 1990. In mid-1989 a bargain hunter could have purchased its shares for less than $12. But by early 1991 the shares had traded as low as $.25—less than 2 percent of its top value in 1987.

First Capital Holdings

The shares of this financial services firm sold at an all-time high of $26.875 in early 1987. In the following years the company invested too heavily in junk bonds and suffered severe erosion in the value of those assets as the junk bond market collapsed. The company was forced into bankruptcy in May, 1991. By that time, the shares had traded at prices under $.10—a decline of more than 99 percent from their top value.

Floating Point Systems

This high-tech company makes computers and related equipment for scientific and engineering applications. In early 1986 the price of its stock peaked at $46.00. Some problems in engineering and with transitions to new product lines resulted in a declining market share and extended loses in the following years. The stock price fell to less than $20.00 a share in the second half of 1986. It may have appeared to be a bargain at that level. However, those who bought then and held on for five years watched the price fall further, to $.375 in early 1991. In September of that year the New York Stock Exchange suspended trading in the shares. The company filed for reorganization under Chapter 11 of the bankruptcy code in October, 1991.

Munsingwear, Inc.

This company makes and sells men's, women's, and children's clothing. The price of its stock reached a high of $18.875 in mid-1986. In subsequent years the company's market share and sales declined, and it began to lose money. A major cash flow problem developed. During the second half of 1987 a bargain hunter could have bought the shares for less than $8.00 each. But this would have been a serious mistake. By late 1990 the shares had declined to $.25—less than 2 percent of the high price.

Prime Motor Inns

This company owns, manages, or operates more than a hundred hotels, motels, and inns. It lent money to some of its units, and experienced severe cash flow problems when the loans were not repaid on time because of a weak travel lodgings market. The price of the stock reached a high of $45.50 in late 1987. In early 1990 bottom fishers could have bought the stock for less than $20.00. But before the end of that year the stock had declined to $.375—less than one percent of its high price. In early 1991 the stock traded at a low of $.25 a share.

Savin Corporation

This company distributes facsimile and copy machines made by Japanese manufacturers. In early 1985 the company's shares reached a price of $9.125. During the rest of the eighties its competitive position eroded, and the company lost money consistently. Bargain hunters could have bought the stock for less than $4.00 a share during 1986. Those who did and held the stock until early 1991 saw the price decline under $.10 per share. The total decline from the peak price was more than 99 percent. This company went bankrupt and was delisted by the New York Stock Exchange in August, 1992.

Tucson Electric Power

This utility company provides electricity to the city of Tucson and its surrounding area. Its stock traded for a high price of $65.00 in mid-1986. The company borrowed heavily to build a new plant to meet an anticipated increase in the demand for power. But when growth in the area slowed, the company was saddled with excess power it was unable to sell to other utilities. By mid-1991 the stock price had declined to $3.50—a paper loss of almost 95 percent from its peak.

U.S. Home

This is one of the largest builders of single-family homes. (Its operations are mainly in the Sunbelt.) In 1983 the price reached a high of $20.75. In the remainder of that decade the single-family housing market growth slowed, and the company lost money most of those years. In 1985 the stock could have been purchased for less than $10.00 a share. Anyone holding the stock until 1991 would have seen the price fall to $.25 per share—a paper loss of more than 98 percent from its high.

BancTexas Group

This is a Dallas based bank holding company. The price of the stock was equivalent to $456.25 in 1981 (after adjustment for a reverse split of one share for 50 in 1987). The company experienced large losses in the mid-eighties with the decline of the oil industry and the commercial real estate market in Texas. By the end of the decade the price of the stock had plunged to $.125 per share—a paper loss of more than 99.9 percent!

Cut Your Losses Short

A person who purchases a "bargain" stock like those described above must act quickly to extricate him or herself from the situation. An investor who buys such a stock and holds onto it too long because he or she is too proud to admit the mistake is subject to huge potential losses of capital and the waste of valuable time.

Note: The examples presented above were selected from stocks whose prices had declined more than ninety-five percent in the 1980s and the early part of the 1990s. They are only a few of the hundreds of companies whose stocks had fallen by more than fifty percent at some point during that period. Some of these companies and the percentage of decline for each are shown in Table 1–2.

Trying to Get Even

Some people refuse to admit to themselves their stock is a loser, even when the evidence is clear. They hold on in the hope the price will come back so they can get out even. Accompanying this hope is an emotional disbelief or denial of the negative aspects of the company's situation. Figure 1–5 gives an example of how a person can waste time while holding on to a loser trying to prove himself or herself right.

This investor heard a takeover rumor about this company and decided to buy in at $62 per share. Other people heard the rumor also and pushed the price to $65. Then the price started to decline. Soon this investor had a paper loss, but decided to hold on, thinking the price couldn't go any lower. Too proud to admit the mistake, this investor watched the price continue to decline. It would be a very long time before the price of this stock would go back to its previous high, if ever.

Table 1–2   Stocks with Major Price Declines

Company Name	High Price & Year		Low Price & Year		Percent of Decline
Atari Corp.	$31.375	'87	$-1.50	'90	95%
Bally Mfg.	29.75	'89	1.87	'91	93
Bank of Boston	38.00	'87	3.00	'91	92
Brunswick Corp.	30.25	'87	6.375	'90	79
Chase Manhattan	49.50	'86	10.25	'91	80
Chrysler Corp.	48.00	'87	9.125	'90	81
Cray Research	135.75	'87	20.00 I	'90	84
Cummins Engine	94.75	'87	31.125	'90	67
Eastman Kodak	71.00	'87	33.75 I	'90	52
Emerson Radio	12.75	'88	2.00	'91	84
Fedders Corp.	18.375	'89	5.00 I	'90	72
General Dynamics	89.25	'86	19.00 I	'90	79
Goodyear Tire	76.50	'87	12.875	'90	83
Knogo Corp.	29.625	'87	6.25	'91	79
Maytag Corp.	32.25	'87	9.875	'90	69
National Semiconductor	22.25	'88	3.00	'90	87
Pier 1 Imports	14.94	'88	3.06	'90	80
Ranger Oil	19.25	'81	2.50	'85	87
Russ Togs	24.125	'88	4.50	'91	81
Ryder Systems	43.00	'87	12.25	'90	72
Travelers Insurance	59.50	'86	11.50	'90	81

Figure 1–5   Trying to Get Even

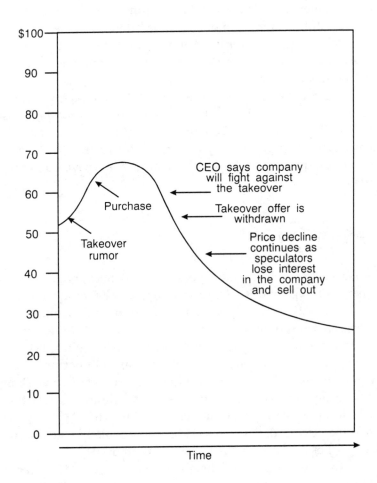

A combination of excessive greed, stubborn pride, and disbelief led this individual into this undesirable situation. A rumor is a poor basis for a purchase. It arouses the desire to make a quick profit, but those who buy on rumors are often disappointed with the results. If the rumor proves to be false, the loss of time and/or money can be extensive. Whether your purchase is based on a rumor or any other reason, staying in a stock because of pride in the hope of getting out even is a self-defeating tactic.

Table 1–3 shows a few examples of the long-term declines which have developed in the stocks of companies which lost their ability to compete. To appreciate just how long one might have to wait to get even, you may wish to check the current quotes on these stocks to see how many have recovered to their previous highs.

Playing the Long Shot

Some aspects of the market appeal to greed. Some brokers try to take advantage of this. Here's an example of how they operate.

A businesswoman received a phone call from a Mr. Hardsell who identified himself as a broker with the firm of Fortune Hunters, Inc. Her interest was piqued, though, because the broker claimed to have a great investment opportunity. His company was selling shares in a bio-tech firm that was working on a genetics project. He offered a brief technical explanation, which the woman did not understand. But when Mr. Hardsell said the price of BioHiTech's shares had doubled in the last two weeks, her desire for a quick profit was aroused.

The current price of the shares was 24¢ bid, 36¢ offered. Mr. Hardsell said the president of BioHiTech met with the brokers at Fortune Hunters Inc. periodically to keep them abreast of progress in the project. (At the last meeting the president had

Table 1–3   Stocks Declining Five Years or Longer

Company Name	High Price & Year	Low Price & Year	Percent of Decline
Armco Steel	$ 41.625 '91	$ 3.875 '91	90%
Caterpillar Inc.	73.25 '81	38.125 '90	48
Continental Bank	171.00 '81	7.125 ;90	96
Control Data	64.375 '83	7.625 '90	88
Data General	76.00 '85	3.50 '90	95
Mitel Corp.	42.00 '81	1.00 '91	98
National Convenience Stores	18.50 '84	2.875 '90	84
Navistar	26.125 '81	2.00 '90	92
Oak Industries	38.50 '81	.375 '90	99
Ocean Drilling & Exploration	50.50 '81	12.50 '88	75
Omnicare	49.50 '83	6.00 '90	88
Oxford Industries	25.75 '84	6.50 '90	75
Pacific Scientific	39.875 '83	7.375 '90	82
Public Service of New Hampshire	20.00 '83	1.75 '90	92
Scientific Atlanta	34.75 '81	8.875 '88	74
Storage Technology	403.75 '81	9.25 '89	98
Sun Electric	29.75 '81	7.375 '91	75
Sunshine Mining	19.125 '83	1.25 '91	93
Tood Shipyards	41.75 '84	1.625 '89	61

predicted the market for the drug his company would manufacture would reach $500 million in a few years.)

Mr. Hardsell urged her to buy BioHiTech quickly before the story was published. She decided to buy one thousand shares since it would cost only a few hundred dollars. Mr. Hardsell advised her to pay the offering price to be certain of making the transaction before the price moved higher. She was anxious to be in on the action so she agreed to do that.

The following week the businesswoman called the broker several times and was delighted to hear that the price had moved up steadily to 40¢ bid, 50¢ offered. The next week Mr. Hardsell quoted a price of 60¢ bid, 70¢ offered. She couldn't believe her good luck. Her money had doubled in just two weeks! Mr. Hardsell urged her to buy more.

She took the bait. She sold her utility stock, cashed in a certificate of deposit and bought ten thousand shares of BioHiTech at 70¢ a share. In the next few weeks the price fluctuated between 75¢ and 95¢. Then the price started to decline. Mr. Hardsell assured her the decline was just a temporary correction and that the price would soon be going up again.

But instead of going up, it gradually declined to 25¢ bid, 35¢ offered. Mr. Hardsell's explanation of a temporary correction was no longer satisfactory. Her profit had disappeared. She was not fearful of losing money; she became very upset. When the price went to 20¢ bid 30¢ offered, her anger at Mr. Hardsell reached the boiling point. She did not sleep well that night. The following morning she called Fortune Hunters to sell her stock and vent her anger at Mr. Hardsell.

The secretary who answered the phone said Mr. Hardsell was no longer with the company. The businesswoman was furious and demanded to speak with the manager. But the manager was "out of town" until next week. When the manager didn't call her back, she called her lawyer, who advised her to sue. A few days later she called Fortune Hunters to tell them they would face a lawsuit if they did not return the money immediately. The telephone company recording said, "Sorry, but that number has been disconnected."

The broker in this story was working for an illegal boiler room operation. Many of these operations are nothing more than temporary offices with banks of telephones. The salespeople who make these calls use deceptive tactics to convince the general public to buy. After the initial sale the salesperson can provide false quotes to the buyer to make him or her think there is a big demand for the stock and that the price is rising fast. But the only demand for the stock is that which is created by the sales force. These operations flourish because some people are susceptible to an appeal to their greed. In the next chapter we will analyze greed and the other emotions that affect many individuals in the stock market.

Chapter 2

Emotions in the Marketplace

The preceding chapter contained examples of how the stock market can elicit emotions. It also demonstrated that emotion-based decisions can have a negative effect on one's financial status.

In this chapter we will review the major emotions in the market to learn how they are detrimental to achieving one's financial objectives. We will see that excessive greed can lure the investor into high-risk investments. We will explore how pride and ego needs can introduce extraneous social considerations into decision making. We will note how love and disbelief can lock an investor into a declining stock. And we will consider the disastrous results of decisions to sell made under conditions of fear or panic.

Greed

Greed is the excessive desire to acquire wealth. Although greed provides much of the vitality in our economic system by motivating people to invest their money, it can produce negative consequences when it overwhelms a person. People who are controlled by greed are not able to establish a proportional balance between risk and reward. They focus their attention on reward but do not see the risk. Ignored risk does not disappear; it's an ever-present potential problem.

How does one know when greed has become the dominant aspect of a transaction and concern for risk has been shunted aside? Table 2–1 outlines some situations in which speculators focus on rewards and ignore financial hazards.

Table 2–1   Hazardous Investments

Speculative Transactions	Financial Hazards
Buying an initial public offering (IPO) in a company which has no recore of earnings .	Many IPOs are used to provide the initial public financing of new or small businesses. This is a high-risk investment until the management of the company can prove its ability to make the company profitable. Department of Commerce reports indicate the great majority of new businesses fail in their first few years of operation.
Buying a stock on the basis of an unsubstantiated rumor of good news	If rumored good news turns out to be false, the price of the stock will probably decline sharply.

Table 2-1   Continued

Speculative Transactions	Financial Hazards
Buying call or put options to speculate on an advance or decline in the underlying equity.	SEC figures show that less than 10 percent of equity option contracts are exercised. Many of the remaining 90 percent are losing contracts. (Some are used by traders to hedge other transactions.) the hazardous feature of options is that they are a wasting asset which becomes worthless on the expiration date.
Buying a stock index option as a speculatin on the rise or fall of the index.	A speculator does not gain or control any equity in buying a call or put on a stock index. He or she is just gambling on a move by the index. The hazardous feature of a stock index option is that it is a wasting asset which becomes worthless on the expiration date.

Table 2–1   Continued

Speculative Transactions	Financial Hazards
Making an uncovered short sale (selling stock short without owning it)	If the price goes into an uptrend, the potentiial loss is unlimited
Buying warrants on the open market when the price of the stock is below the exercise price and there are less than a couple of months to expiration date	The chance of making a profit in the transaction declines with the passage of time. One may have no choice but to sell the warrants at a loss before they expire.
Buying a stock which has run up in price on the basis of a takeover attempt	If the attempt fails, the price is likely to decline quickly.
Buying a stock listed on the pink sheets	Since only a few dealers make a market in many of these stocks, an orderly market can not be assured. Bid and asked spreads are often large, and the buyer has a sizeable paper loss right after the purchase.

Table 2–1   Continued

Speculative Transactions

Buying shares in a blind pool

Financial Hazards

Your money can be put to any speculative use by the pool organizer. Most of this venture capital finances new companies which have untested managers producing new or experimental products or services for which a market must be developed. The risk factor in these pools is very high.

Hi Rollers Get Lucky Sometimes

Note that some high-risk investments do work out well. A sophisticated investor who understands the danger can make a large profit with a properly timed and selected speculation. Moreover, some people do make good profits in high-risk transactions by sheer luck. However, if a friend or business associate boasts about his or her success in a hazardous investment, don't let the story stimulate your greed.

Here are two additional suggestions for resisting the temptation to speculate in a hazardous situation. First, keep in mind that a lucky transaction may easily be followed by an unlucky one. Second, recognize that when your friends boast about their profits from high-risk speculations, your prudent reaction is to let them brag. When their luck changes for the worse, it'll be their problem—not yours.

Here are some guidelines to help protect you against the hazards of ignoring risks:

1. Recognize there is some degree of risk associated with every investment in the market.

2. Before making any investment, spend the time and effort to identify the risk and to assess it. Note: the *Value Line Investment Survey* (see Appendix A, *References and Information Sources*) provides a means for assessing the risks associated with ownership of 1,700 individual stocks. This service ranks each of these stocks in one of five categories from the safest to the riskiest, and identifies those which have the highest safety rating.

3. When you determine that the risk factor is high, commit only a small fraction of your assets—those you can afford to lose.

4. When you are not able to evaluate the risk, don't make the investment.

5. If the investment is a complex one you don't fully understand, it will be difficult, if not impossible, for you to assess the risk. Avoid this type of investment.

Pride

Pride is the satisfaction or delight some people experience when the stock they bought goes up. They have reason to feel proud, but how they react to the feeling determines its ultimate effect on their decision-making ability.

People react in either of two ways. They either feel a quiet, private satisfaction, or they try to impress their friends by making references to their paper profits. If a person chooses the latter course of action, the ego becomes involved in the situation. a person who is ego-involved with the price of a stock complicates decision making unnecessarily. Let's review the complications from two perspectives: when the price is moving up and when it's moving down.

In the bull phase of price movement the individual will be eager to talk about the investment. He or she will take credit for a smart selection and may boast about the paper profit. In addition to the objective of making a profit, he or she will be concerned with impressing friends. This consideration may cause the investor to hold on too long.

What happens if the individual doesn't sell at the top, and the price declines? He or she may feel a loss of prestige in the opinion of friends. The individual would hope for a recovery to prove the wisdom of the investment, and to salvage the ego. In this situation the individual experiences the double pressures of worrying both about the declining profit and what friends will think if the sale is made lower than the top or at a loss.

Some people also complicate the decision-making process by making predictions about the price action of stocks they hold. When a person tells friends or associates a stock will rise to a certain price, his or her ego is on the line.

To avoid these unnecessary complications, enjoy your stock market successes with quiet, private pride. Don't boast about your profits and don't make price predictions. Don't handicap your efforts by making yourself vulnerable to unnecessary embarrassment. The stock market has been known to humiliate those who publicize their stock market achievements because of ego or pride.

Love

While a person cannot fall in love with a stock in the traditional sense, one can develop a strong liking for it and an unwillingness to part company. How does one become attached to a stock?

The affair may start when you buy a stock that is just beginning a sustained upward move in price. In the months that follow there is much good news about the company. The earnings are rising. The dividend is increased, and price reversals are shallow and short lived. If the prosperity of the company lasts for a long time, your attachment to it increases. You have a pleasant feeling every time you think about how good the stock has been. In view of the stock's excellent performance, the thought of welling it might seem like disloyalty. As with greed, love can blind a person to the risk element.

What are some clues that you could be in love with a stock? You often praise the stock to your friends and associates. The price has multiplied since you bought, and you're expecting continuous price increases. You have a personal attachment to the company and would feel disloyal if you sold.

Loving a company and its stock is not a problem as long as its price advances to meet your expectations. Or perhaps you bought the stock for income. If the company pays a good dividend and raises it periodically, there's no harm in loving the stock. You have good reason to hold these types of stocks as long as these conditions persist.

But you should not let your love blind you to the probability that these favorable conditions will not last forever. When they come to a reversal point, you should be prepared to end your love affair.

For some investors, a love affair can develop into euphoria. If the price of the stock goes up beyond investors' wildest dreams, they become euphoric. They may experience sheer joy and a psychological high as a result of finding such an easy way to make money. It doesn't occur to them that paper profits can disappear as quickly as they materialized. The idea of risk is gone. The cardinal rule that you shouldn't count your winnings until you leave the table has been forgotten.

Disbelief

Disbelief is refusing to admit the price of a stock is actually declining after a long rise. the stockholder can't accept that a stock which has done so well could turn around and do this. As far as this person is concerned, the price of the stock has every reason to continue rising. The prospects for the company are good. Earnings are growing. There are probably some advisory services which recommend it be bought. Company officials may speak of its future in glowing terms. (Unfortunately, the price of the stock may have already discounted these factors.)

The disbelieving person looks for reasons why the decline should not be taken seriously. For example, it's a temporary aberration caused by some fund selling a large holding—just a short-term decline that must end soon. Self-deceptive efforts such as these continue until this person can no longer deny something has changed for the worse. For a while it was possible to deny the bitter truth because the change occurred while the prospects for the company appeared to be so positive. The cause of the change, though not apparent, was simple.

The price of the stock had risen so high that additional buyers willing to pay that much were far outnumbered by the sellers. The supply of shares available for sale became much greater than the amount sought for purchase. As sellers realized this, they lowered their offering prices and were willing to accept less. Potential buyers also noted the new weakness in demand and lowered their bids. As the price moved lower and lower, the stubborn disbeliever eventually had to face reality and deal with some difficult questions.

Should the stock be sold at these lower prices? Will the stock ever go back to its peak price again? Should the stockholder wait for a partial comeback? How much lower might the price go?

Confronted by these uncertainties, what was formerly a joy has become a worry. When the price is checked, it is usually lower. The party is over.

Fear

The insecurity and nervousness caused by an extended downward movement in the price of a stock can develop into fear. The investor becomes frightened that the price will go even lower. The larger the percent of assets the stockholder has invested in the stock, the more fearful he or she becomes.

A sustained decline in price presents the investor with a severe test of fortitude. The individual wonders how this happened. Why didn't he or she have the foresight to sell at the higher price? Without good answers to these questions, the fear increases. Unable to foretell the future, there's no way for the investor to derive any comfort in this situation.

After a while one may hear some negative rumors about the company. Should one believe them? Should one wait to see what management has to say? (It may be a long while before management says anything because they often delay releasing bad news.)

The stockholder may also face another aggravating question. Will the price start rising right after the sale is made? The uncertainties generated by these unknowns make any decision difficult. The stockholder may feel like a non-swimmer drifting down a river toward a steep waterfall. Faced with an unpleasant situation and with no clue to the best solution to the problem, the stockholder may feel overwhelmed.

Panic

When a stock declines a long distance because of bad news about the company, a stockholder has good reason to be disheartened. There are few events more demoralizing than seeing your investment plunge in value. As a stock approaches a bottom, the price may go into a free fall, wherein the price goes down without letup for a while. When this happens, a feeling of despair can take over, and all hope for recovery is lost.

The stockholder agonizes over the question, "How low can the price go?" The answer seems to be, "Much further than imagined." Perhaps there are rumors the company will be forced into bankruptcy because it can't pay the interest on its debt. If so, the investor may become frantic. Everything could be lost if the company goes bankrupt!

The idea that the money invested could be lost completely can precipitate a feeling of panic. The stockholder becomes so desperate to sell that he or she feels compelled to take whatever is offered for the stock. After giving the broker an order to "sell at the market," the investor is appalled by the low price received.

Impact of Euphoria and Panic in the Stock Market

Euphoria or panic can also play a major role in the psychology of the general public. Euphoria is the dominant emotion affecting many investors and speculators as a bull market approaches its peak. In the euphoric phase the market averages are rising fast, and the economy looks strong. People are optimistic and self-confident. This feeling will be especially strong among the new investors who are experiencing their first bull market.

All types of stocks are rising: blue chips, growth, high-tech, cyclical, conservative, and speculative. almost everyone believes the market is going much higher. Money flows into it from other forms of investment. But a bull market doesn't last forever. Too many people borrow money to speculate in the market. The abundance of cash, credit, and demand pushes prices to unrealistic heights until the advance can no longer be sustained. Finally, selling pressure overcomes buying pressure. As the overbought market makes its top, the euphoria fades away.

The opposite emotion, panic, often develops as a bear market approaches a bottom. Gloom is everywhere. The newspapers, magazines, and commentators dwell on the poor condition of the economy and the terrible performance of the market. As it declines, people lose confidence. Margin calls wipe out those who have borrowed too much. There's very little new money coming into the market, and prices plunge. Short-term traders and speculators wish they had sole their holdings at much higher levels. Such panic conditions often end in a selling climax, after which the market begins to form a base for the next bull phase.

Chapter 3

 # Identifying Your Emotional Decisions

In Chapter 2 we analyzed the emotions which are found in the marketplace. If you've been investing in the market, you may be subject to these emotions. The purpose of this chapter is to help you determine the extent to which your buy, hold, and sell decisions are affected by these feelings. This evaluation will be accomplished by means of an exercise which focuses on your emotional responses to stock market events, rumors, and stock price movements.

Why Should You Do This Exercise?

1. If you made too many losing transactions, this exercise will help you discover if emotional components are interfering with your decision-making process.

2. If you have been trading frequently, but making little or no profit, it could be that feelings of greed, fear, and panic are driving much of this non-productive activity. (The same situation could apply if your trading is resulting in losses.)

3. If you have bought stocks which decline soon after your purchase, excessive greed may be one of the causes.

4. If you have been holding stocks after they have made tops and declined sharply, it may be because of blind love and a refusal to believe the fundamental outlook for the companies have worsened.

5. If you have been holding some stocks for long periods, waiting for them to rise to the price you paid, you may be doing so because of stubborn pride.

6. If you have regretted making sales because the prices rose afterwards, you may have been pressured to sell by feelings of fear and panic near the bottom.

In each of these situations you have a chance to improve your performance if you can identify the emotional driving forces and learn to control them. For this reason, it's crucial that you be completely honest with yourself when doing the following exercise, since it's impossible to change something you are not aware of. Only after you have acknowledged any emotions in your decision making, will you be able to learn how to control them in your transactions.

Exercise Procedure

There are three steps to the exercise.
— One, gathering information on your past transactions and current holdings.
— Two, reviewing your reasons for purchasing, selling, and holding each item to identify any emotional components.
— Three, calculating your Emotion Quotient (a simple division of one number by another which provides a quotient rang-

ing between zero and one hundred percent). This calculation will give you an estimate of the emotional component in your decision making.

Step #1, Gathering the Data

Collect information on each transaction you made in the last seven years. The transactions to be included in this list are purchases or sales of

- ◆ stocks

- ◆ stock purchase rights

- ◆ warrants

- ◆ stock options

- ◆ stock index options

Note: Short sales are not included in this exercise because the details and mechanics are too complicated. Short sales can be done for speculation on the decline in price of a stock, as a tax deferral tactic, as a hedge to reduce risk, as a component of an arbitrage strategy, etc. Since they are often done in combination with other transactions, it is difficult to determine if emotions played a role in selling short or in covering the sale. In the interest of keeping the exercise simple, short sales have therefore been excluded.

Similarly, any other purchase or sale which does not stand alone as an independent transaction should be excluded from step one, information gathering.

The information on purchases and sales is in your Federal Income Tax reports, Schedule D. Information on current holdings appears in your most recent account statement from your broker, unless you are holding your certificates. Post this information on the worksheet in this chapter.

This worksheet has two pages for posting 40 purchases, two pages for posting 40 sales, and two for posting 40 items you are currently holding. There's no need to post more than those amounts.

For each entry, post the name of the company or the stock index and the type of investment instrument. For example:

General Motors: Common stock

General Motors: Call option

General Motors: Put option

General Motors: Rights

General Motors: Warrants

Standard and Poor's 100 stock index: Call option

Standard and Poor's 500 stock index: Put option

N.Y. Stock Exchange Index: Call option

AMEX Institutional Index: Put option

After you finish posting your purchases, sales, and holdings, proceed to the next step.

Step #2, Part One: Reviewing Your Purchases

Review the following list of reasons for purchasing—all of which contain an element of excessive greed. Then review each of your purchases. As you conduct this review, enter a check mark in the appropriate space provided.

1. You bought after getting a hot tip the price would have a large rise on information that hadn't been published yet.

2. Someone who works in the company said she couldn't tell you the reason, but told you to buy the stock for a quick profit.

3. You bought a stock listed on the pink sheets because the price was only a few cents a share, and you were told the price would rise sharply.

4. Your broker said she was trying to put all her clients into the stock because she heard it was ready for a big rise.

5. A financial commentator said the company was the subject of a takeover rumor.

6. Your broker sold you these shares in this new company, which he claimed would have a fast run-up in price.

7. The market has been making record highs for months. You called your broker and asked him to recommend a hot stock. He suggested this one.

8. This low-priced stock was touted to be the next Home Depot, Disney, or AmGen.

9. You were convinced a market was about to rally, so you bought a call option on this stock index.

10. You were convinced the market was vulnerable to a steep drop, so you bought a put option on this stock index.

11. You bought a stock listed on the pink sheets because you heard they planned to push the price much higher.

12. Your broker recommended a blind pool, so you bought into it, hoping to take a quick profit.

13. Although these stock purchase rights were scheduled to expire in two weeks, you bought them because the price was rising.

14. You had a hunch the stock price was going to rise fast, so you bought these warrants.

15. You had a hunch the stock price would rise fast, so you bought a call option.

16. You had a hunch the stock price would fall fast, so you bought a put option.

17. You bought this stock listed on the pink sheets because a friend had a large profit in it and claimed it would go much higher.

18. You bought this stock on the basis of a phone call from a broker you didn't know. He said the price was moving up fast and claimed your investment would multiply in a few months.

19. You bought this stock after seeing it trade actively on the ticker tape. You had never heard of the company, but you figured something was happening because the price was rising fast.

Step #2, Part Two: Reviewing Your Sales

Review the following list of reasons for selling—all of which contain an element of fear or panic. Then review each of your sales to see which ones reflect any of these reasons. As you conduct this review, enter a check mark in the appropriate space.

1. You had a large paper loss and were afraid the price would go even lower.

2. The Dow Jones Industrial Average went into a free fall, and all your acquaintances were selling.

3. You went bottom fishing, but were surprised to see the price go much lower after you bought.

4. The company announced bad news. The price went into a free fall, and you were frightened.

5. You bought this stock at a much higher price. When the price went below a dollar a share, you decided to throw in the towel.

6. The company released bad news. The exchange suspended trading in the stock. When it started trading again, you were dismayed the price had dropped so much.

7. You bought when you heard a takeover rumor, but the deal fell apart and the price dropped fast.

8. When a financial commentator reported a rumor that the company would file for bankruptcy, you panicked.

9. The price had been declining for several months, and you couldn't stand the stress of watching it go down.

10. There was no news on this company, but the price dropped several points quickly. You didn't know what was happening and were frightened.

11. You already had a large paper loss in the stock . . . then the price went into a free fall. You panicked.

12. These stock purchase rights were scheduled to expire in a few days. The pressure became unbearable; you decided to take the loss before the rights became worthless.

13. These warrants were drifting lower, and you saw no chance to sell and break even before the expiration date. You decided to take the loss rather than lose everything.

14. You had a large percentage paper loss on this call option, which would have expired in a few weeks.

15. You had a large percentage paper loss on this put option, which would have expired in a few weeks.

Step #2, Part Three: Reviewing Your Current Holdings

Review the following list of reasons for holding. Then review each of your holdings. As you conduct this review, enter a check mark in the appropriate space.

Reasons for holding based on an element of greed, price, love, or disbelief:

1. You have a paper loss in this stock, but you won't sell until you can receive the price you paid.

2. This is your best performing stock. You're proud of it and are recommending it to all your friends.

3. You have a paper loss on this put option. You're hoping you won't have to sell it at a loss before it expires.

4. You have a paper loss on this option. It expires in a few months, and you're trying to decide whether to take the loss or keep hoping for the price to recover.

5. The CEO of this company predicted record profits for the next few years, but since the prediction was made a few months ago, the stock price has been declining. You still have a paper profit and believe the price drop is temporary.

6. You have a paper loss in these stock purchase rights. They expire in a few days, and you're trying to decide whether to take the loss, or hope for a recovery.

7. The price of this stock has multiplied several times since you bought. You're convinced the price will keep multiplying, so you wouldn't think of selling it.

8. You have a paper loss in this stock. The dividend provides a high return on your investment, so you don't see how the price can go any lower.

9. You bought this stock after it was recommended by a friend. The price rose for a while, but now you have a loss. You don't believe the price will drop further.

10. This is stock in the company where you work. the large profit you had is gone, but you won't sell because you would feel disloyal.

11. You've had these warrants for several years and have a paper loss. The warrants have several more years before they expire, and you refuse to sell at a loss.

12. After you bought this stock, the price rose for a couple of years. But then the price stalled, fluctuated up and down for more than a year, then declined. Now you have a loss, but you believe the price will move up again.

13. You have a paper loss in this call option on a stock index. You're waiting for the market to rally to prove you were right.

14. This penny stock is almost worthless now. You're too embarrassed to tell your broker to sell because the size of the check would be so small compared to what you paid.

15. You've held this stock for a few years. At first the company did well and paid a reliable dividend. Then they cut the dividend in half. You have a paper loss now, but you're not going to sell until you can get out even.

Step #3, Calculating Your Emotion Quotient

(Use page seven of the worksheet to calculate your Emotion Quotient.)

Emotion Quotient Worksheet
Page #1, Items Purchased

Description of Item Purchased

**Enter Checkmark Below If
Emotion Was Involved**

_____   _____

_____   _____

_____   _____

_____   _____

_____   _____

_____   _____

_____   _____

_____   _____

_____   _____

_____   _____

_____   _____

_____   _____

_____   _____

_____   _____

_____   _____

_____   _____

_____   _____

_____   _____

Emotion Quotient Worksheet
Page #2, Items Purchased (Continued)

Description of Item Purchased

**Enter Checkmark Below If
Emotion Was Involved**

_____   _____

_____   _____

_____   _____

_____   _____

_____   _____

_____   _____

_____   _____

_____   _____

_____   _____

_____   _____

_____   _____

_____   _____

_____   _____

_____   _____

_____   _____

_____   _____

_____   _____

_____   _____

Emotion Quotient Worksheet
Page #3, Items Sold

Description of Item Sold

**Enter Checkmark Below If
Emotion Was Involved**

_____   _____

_____   _____

_____   _____

_____   _____

_____   _____

_____   _____

_____   _____

_____   _____

_____   _____

_____   _____

_____   _____

_____   _____

_____   _____

_____   _____

Emotion Quotient Worksheet
Page #4, Items Sold (Continued)

Description of Item Sold

**Enter Checkmark Below If
Emotion Was Involved**

_____   _____

_____   _____

_____   _____

_____   _____

_____   _____

_____   _____

_____   _____

_____   _____

_____   _____

_____   _____

_____   _____

_____   _____

_____   _____

_____   _____

_____   _____

_____   _____

_____   _____

_____   _____

Emotion Quotient Worksheet
Page #5, Items Currently Held

Description of Item Held

**Enter Checkmark Below If
Emotion Was Involved**

_____   _____

_____   _____

_____   _____

_____   _____

_____   _____

_____   _____

_____   _____

_____   _____

_____   _____

_____   _____

_____   _____

_____   _____

_____   _____

_____   _____

_____   _____

_____   _____

_____   _____

Emotion Quotient Worksheet
Page #6, Items Currently Held (Continued)

Description of Item Held

**Enter Checkmark Below If
Emotion Was Involved**

_____	_____
_____	_____
_____	_____
_____	_____
_____	_____
_____	_____
_____	_____
_____	_____
_____	_____
_____	_____
_____	_____
_____	_____
_____	_____
_____	_____
_____	_____
_____	_____

Emotion Quotient Worksheet
Page #7, Calculating Your Emotion Quotient

Total the number of check marks you made on the six worksheets and enter the total here. _____

Total the number of items listed on the six worksheets and enter the total here. _____

Divide the number of check marks by the number of items listed and enter the result here. _____

Now convert the decimal figure to a percentage and enter your Emotion Quotient here. _____%

> Example: Number of check marks equals 50.
>
> Number of items equals 100.
>
> 50 divided by 100 equals .50.
>
> Converted to a percentage, this gives an Emotion Quotient of 50 percent.

Interpreting Emotion Quotients

Now that you have calculated your Emotion Quotient, what does it mean?

— If your quotient was 20 percent or lower, you have excellent control over emotional reactions in your stock market transactions. A quotient between 20 percent and 40 percent signifies good control. A quotient between 40 percent and 60 percent indicates medium control. A quotient between 60 percent and 80 percent reflects poor control. A quotient above 80 percent means lack of control.

— If you are not satisfied with your performance in the market and your Emotion Quotient is 40 percent or higher, you have much to gain by initiating an effort to increase your control over the various emotions which may be having a negative impact on the results you are achieving.

— If you are not satisfied with your performance in the market and your Emotion Quotient is between 20 percent and 40 percent, improving your results will depend both on increasing your emotional control and your ability to select investments.

— If you are not satisfied with your performance in the market and your Emotion Quotient is below 20 percent, improved results will be largely dependent upon increasing your ability to select investments.

Table 3–1 is provided as a guide for interpreting and applying your Emotional Quotient. However, its purpose is not to prevent you from following your personal needs.

For example, if your Emotion Quotient is between 0 percent and 40 percent and you want both capital gains and current income, you could select a growth and income fund instead of a growth fund.

Recommended Follow-Up Procedure

If your current Emotion Quotient is higher than 20 percent, you should perform an annual review to check on your progress in reducing it until you have achieved excellent control over your emotional reactions. Table 3–2 will allow you to record your progress in the next several years.

After calculating your current score, enter it on the line labeled "Initial Emotion Quotient" in Table 3–2. When your bro-

Table 3-1   Emotion Quotient Application Guide

E.Q. Score	Suggested Investment Limit	Suggested Risk Level	Some Investment Alternatives
Above 80%	10% of discretionary funds	Low	Index or Growth/Income fund
60% to 80%	20 % of discretionary funds	Low	Index or Growth/Income fund
40% to 60%	30% of discretionary funds	Medium	Index, Growth, or Growth/Income fund: blue chips
20% to 40%	40% of discretionary funds	Within comfort zone	Index or Growth fund; growth or blue chip stocks
Up to 20%	50% of discretionary funds or more if within comfort zone	Within comfort zone	Growth or Sector fund; growth or blue chip stocks; also cyclicals if using buy & sell strategy

ker sends you the statement of activity and status of your account for each subsequent year, calculate another Emotion Quotient and enter it on the line specified for that year. (A lined pad formatted after the fashion of the preceding worksheet will provide means for recording the data to calculate the follow-up Emotion Quotients.)

This follow-up procedure will keep you aware of your progress in achieving control over your emotional reactions to events in the market, and give you the satisfaction of seeing the results of your self-improvement efforts.

Table 3–2   Record of Emotion Quotients

Initial Emotion Quotient: _____%

Follow-up Emotion Quotients:
for subsequent years

      1st _____

      2nd _____

      3rd _____

      4th_____

      5th_____

      6th_____

      7th_____

      8th_____

      9th_____

      10th_____

Chapter 4

Developing Control over Emotions

After doing the exercise in Chapter 3 you may have concluded you need to exert more control over the emotions you experience in your market dealings. Developing this control will require additional self-analysis and some corrective actions. Depending on the amount of self-control you need to develop, this could be a short-, intermediate- or long-term effort.

This chapter describes the factors which can lead to stress and emotional reactions. They are social competitiveness, over-extension, ignorance of risk, unrealistic expectations, and over-confidence. Questions are provided to help you estimate your susceptibility to each one.

The final sections of the chapter provide a framework for counteracting those factors and for dealing with each of the emotions. The symptoms and hazards of each emotion are described. Being alert to those symptoms and aware of the associated hazards will help you prevent or resolve the emotional reactions you may be subject to.

Social Competitiveness

The stock market provides an arena for competition. Some people invest not only to make money but to prove they are better at it than others. They want to be more accurate at predicting the direction of the market and individual stocks. They want to make larger paper profits and capital gains than their friends and associates.

Do you feel competitive in regard to your performance in the market in comparison to how others are doing? Do you view the market as a place to demonstrate your money-making ability to your friends and associates? Do you feel dissatisfied with your gains in the market when one of your friends or associates is doing better than you are?

The trouble with this socially competitive attitude is that it results in feelings of pride or shame. When such an investor is doing better than friends and associates, he or she feels proud. This pride can lead the investor to take actions which are counterproductive. It can induce a person to hold a stock too long because of his or her public commitment. It can motivate an individual to trade frequently in a search for faster rising stocks. (Such in and out trading often results in higher commissions rather than larger profits.) Concerns about how your friends will react to your profits or losses should not be allowed to affect your thinking.

On the other hand, when a socially competitive investor is doing worse than friends and associates, he or she must struggle with feelings of shame and embarrassment. These feelings will be especially keen if the investor is losing money while others are making profits. And these feelings can also cloud the investor's thought processes.

Thus, whether ahead or behind others, the socially competitive investor is handicapped in dealing with the emotional challenges of the market. Maintaining the privacy of activities in the market allows the investor to focus his or her mental efforts on achieving financial goals.

Overextension

Another cause of emotion in the market is investing too much. Even worse is borrowing money to buy stocks. A person who is overextended in the market is likely to experience satisfaction when his or her stocks are moving up, but when they're going down, this feeling may be replaced by fear or panic. The thought of losing money, especially borrowed money, can be a fearful prospect.

Do you

◆ invest amounts that make you feel vulnerable?

◆ feel nervous when your stock declines?

◆ worry about how you will pay back a loan you obtained to purchase stock?

◆ have a feeling of despair when you think about a large paper loss on a stock?

It's possible to prevent these symptoms of overextension by becoming sensitive to your comfort zone. To determine how much money to invest in the stock market, ask yourself if you would be upset if you lost it. If the answer is yes, the amount is too much. If you want to borrow money to increase the size of your investment, ask yourself if you will be able to repay the loan easily if the investment turns out to be a loser. If not, don't borrow the money.

Risk Ignorance

Investors who are controlled by greed can become blind to the factor of risk. These investors find it far more pleasurable to think about profits than to concern themselves with the painful thought that they might lose money instead. A prudent investor understands the basic reality of the reward-to-risk relationship. Investments with potential for high rewards generally involve high risks.

Investors who take on high reward/high risk investments without assessing the risk factor put themselves in emotionally vulnerable positions. If the investment declines in value, they are taken by surprise and tend to react with fear or panic.

In making investments have you ever done any of the following?:

◆ focused mainly on the possibilities for profit?

◆ assumed you could tolerate whatever risk might be involved in high-profit investments?

◆ found it difficult to resist when your broker or a tipster offered a chance to invest in a "sure thing"?

◆ been taken by surprise and panicked when a "sure thing" investment resulted in a large loss?

Risk must be assessed before each investment. By avoiding high- risk situations or limiting the amount invested, you can protect yourself against large financial losses and stressful emotional reactions.

Unrealistic Expectations

Some inexperienced investors view the stock market as a place to acquire riches quickly. Their expectations of success are unrealistically high. For example, an unsophisticated person might buy a stock at $1.00 a share because he or she expects it to go to $50.00 a share. While this is possible, the chance is small. It's more likely that a low price stock will do nothing, or go down.

Some people open margin accounts because they believe the extra leverage will produce profits more quickly. They don't realize the leverage works in both directions, and losses increase more quickly also. Others buy stocks on hunches, whims, or the self-delusion they can pick winners easily.

Do you

- ◆ think that investing in one stock will make you rich?

- ◆ buy a stock because you don't want to miss the "opportunity of lifetime"?

- ◆ invest a lot of money in a stock you just heard about because you don't want to miss the boat?

- ◆ think leverage is a one-way street to riches?

Expectations and actions such as these set you up for disappointment and make you vulnerable to emotional reactions. It's difficult to maintain emotional stability when you see your $1.00 stock go to 50¢, receive a margin call when your assets are depleted, or watch the stock you rushed to buy on a hunch go into a long decline.

Overconfidence

The four factors described above operate throughout the market cycle. But during a long, powerful bull market another factor comes into play. This is bull-market-nurtured overconfidence.

As a new bull market starts upward, it fosters the development of certain attitudes and feelings in new investors. Rising prices give them a feeling of prosperity. Their self-confidence may change to overconfidence as the stocks they buy gain in value. They may become convinced they have a natural talent for picking winners. They see their success in accumulating paper profits as evidence of their expertise in the market and even offer investment advice to their friends.

As the upward movement of the market continues, they make assumptions about how much further it will rise. These assumptions are based on a straight-line projection that the market will keep rising indefinitely. With the large gains in their portfolios, their attention becomes focused on the potential for additional gains, and as the market approaches its peak, their romance with their stocks blossoms into affection and love. have you ever stayed in a stock because of an unrealistic projection as to how high it would go?

Have you ever held a stock that skyrocketed and then crashed back to earth?

Have you ever said, "If I had sold that stock at the top, I would have made a fortune"?

An overconfident investor who has fallen in love with a company does not see developing problems and doesn't accept the possibility of a reversal of fortune. Positive feelings toward a high performance stock are understandable. But the prudent investor watches for fundamental changes in the prospects for each company.

Some signs the alert investor looks for are shrinking market share, declining earnings from operations, or the assumption of excess debt in relation to other companies in that industry. (This type of information is reported in *The Wall Street Journal, Investor's Daily* newspaper, and other financial publications.) Maintaining this objective, critical attitude toward your stock holdings can protect you against the hazards of overconfidence.

Framework for Developing Emotional Control

An approach which can help you develop emotional stability in your market dealings contains three elements: good timing, low risk, and limits on the amount invested.

The first and foremost element of this approach—good timing—is to wait for the market to decline to a bottom before making purchases. The four stages of a market cycle are: upward movement, making a top, downward movement, and making a bottom. (On the average market, cycles take between four and five years to complete themselves.) By being patient you'll achieve some important objectives on the road to emotional stability. Having paid minimal prices for your stock, you'll be less likely to see the price decline below what you paid. This safety margin will help you handle the stress of seeing a major decline in your paper profits if you use a strategy of buy and hold for the long run.

The second element of the approach is to give preference to low- or medium-risk investments. Avoiding high-risk investments is extremely important because it reduces your chances of becoming entangled in emotionally stressful situations. (Some low risk and medium risk investments are listed in Table 3–1.)

The third element of the approach is to limit your investment to an amount within your comfort zone, which you are willing to leave invested for an indefinite time period. If you are under no pressure to reclaim this money, it will have ample time to appreciate. And it will be easier for you to remain patient.

Avoiding Market Bottom Panic

For some investors, the approach of a market bottom induces a panic reaction. It can be the straw which breaks the camel's back. An understanding of the characteristics of market bottoms will help you resist the urge to panic and sell out during that phase of the market cycle.

Market bottoms take on different forms. Some are made quickly and others can take many months. One type of bottom represents the final capitulation of many investors to a bear market which has been in effect for the preceding months. These investors become exhausted from watching the erosion of their capital. As their paper losses grow, they develop pessimism about the future prospects for stocks. Finally, they decide they can't take any more and initiate a massive wave of selling. When this selling wave subsides, a new bull market begins. This exceptionally high volume trading after a long period of declining prices is called a selling climax.

It will help to maintain emotional stability during a selling climax if you are aware that such market bottoms are generally completed in less than three days. If you can control your fears during this short period, you can convert the atmosphere of disaster into an opportunity to make purchases at extremely low prices.

On the other hand, some market bottoms take a much longer time to complete themselves—from a few weeks to many months. Instead of receiving much publicity, the market is out of the news. The typical investor has lost interest in stocks because not much is happening. Trading volume has declined, and price changes are small. The market is quietly forming a base for its next rise.

In these slowly developing situations the prudent investor has to exercise patience and outlast the dull market. While the prices won't be as low as during a selling climax, some of the equity funds, individual blue chips, and growth stocks will be available at bargain prices.

Whether the market bottoms out quickly or slowly, your ability to resist the pressure to sell out near the bottom is one of the keys to long-term investment success. Avoiding competitiveness, high risk stocks, excessive expectations, and overextending yourself will help you in this test of fortitude.

Table 4–1 presents a summary of suggestions for dealing with emotions. It outlines the symptoms you can observe in yourself to alert you to potentially hazardous situations. The recommended precautions and solutions can help limit your exposure to unnecessary losses.

Table 4–1   Suggestions for Dealing with Emotions

Emotion	Symptoms and Characteristics	Related Problem or Hazard	Precaution or Solution
Uncontrolled greed	Attention is focused on the reward. Risk is ignored.	Little or no concern about potential loss.	Check *Value Line* safety ranking to assess risk before buying. Avoid risky stocks or limit amount invested.
Public pride	Boasting about your stock. Predicting further price rise to others.	Ego is exposed to embarrassment. Staying with a stagnant stock to prove you are right.	Enjoy success privately. Don't predict price rise to friends or associates.
Unquestioning love	Believing the stock should not be sold. Feeling you would be disloyal to sell.	Unrealistic opinion the price will rise indefinitely.	Read *Wall Street Journal* to see if company's profit margin is declining or market share is shrinking. If so, consider selling.
Stubborn disbelief	Refusing to believe a decline in price can continue.	Paper profit shrinks and may disappear. Assets are exposed to large losses.	Recognize that what goes up will come down someday.
Paralyzing fear	Feeling dismayed and frightened by current paper loss and open to more losses.	Indecision about which will be the lesser of two evils—holding or selling.	Force yourself to choose: sell while the loss is small, or hold and hope for price to recover.
Panic reaction	Feeling of despair and impending disaster.	An urge to sell out for whatever you can get.	Hold on and hope for eventual recovery if company has a chance of survival.

Chapter 5

 # Investment
Strategies

Over the long term the stock market as represented by the Dow Jones Industrial Average (DJIA), has followed a persistent upward trend. In 1940 the DJIA was less than 150. The high for the year 1990 was 3,000. This is an increase of two thousand percent in fifty years. Few other investments have such an impressive record. Although the stock market is an attractive vehicle for seeking long-term capital gains, there's no guarantee that similar results will be achieved in the next fifty years.

Market Volatility and Emotional Stress

While the market has this high potential for rewards, it does not rise in a smooth, straight line. There will be downward movements that a long-term investor must learn to deal with if he or she is to be successful. Figure 5–1 illustrates hypothetical market fluctuations including potential periods of stress over the long run.

An individual can select from several market strategies to profit from this long-term uptrend. Diagrammatic representations of three such strategies appear on the following pages.

Figure 5–1   Hypothetical Market Fluctuation

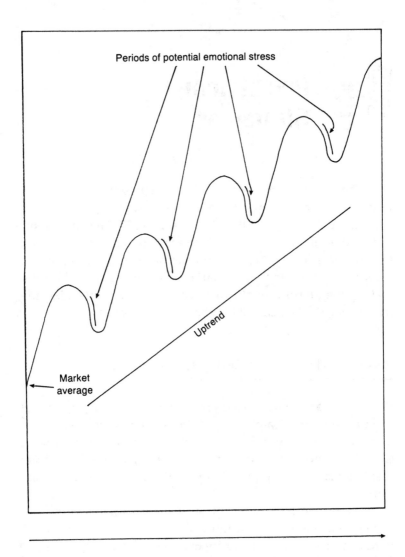

Strategy #1: Buy and Hold

General Description

The objective of the buy and hold strategy is to make long-term capital gains. An individual new to the market can implement this strategy even though he or she may have little knowledge of how to select stocks for the long-term. One way to do this is to buy shares in a growth-oriented fund and let the management of the fund do the stock selection and timing of purchases for you. Another method is to purchase shares in a stock index fund. (The managers of these funds purchase only those stocks which are in one of the major stock indices or averages, such as the Standard and Poor's 100 stock index.) The investor buying into one of these funds is therefore assured that his or her capital gains will approximate those made by that market index or average. A more experienced investor can make his or her own stock selections, to seek to outperform the market averages in the long run. Thus, this strategy can be employed by any investor—from one just starting to invest in the market to one who has extensive experience.

Emotion Control Requirements

The most difficult part of this strategy for both experienced and inexperienced investors is learning to handle two strong emotions: fear and panic. These emotions may occur during the emotionally stressful downtrends. If your Emotion Quotient is higher than 40 percent, it is important for you to be prepared for this potential problem.

Timing your initial purchase so as enter the market after it has made a bottom is the best tactic for keeping this stress to a minimum. Chapter 6 outlines the chart patterns which occur at market bottoms. Studying these patterns will help you to make your purchases at appropriate points in the market cycles.

Figure 5–2   Strategy #1, Buy and Hold

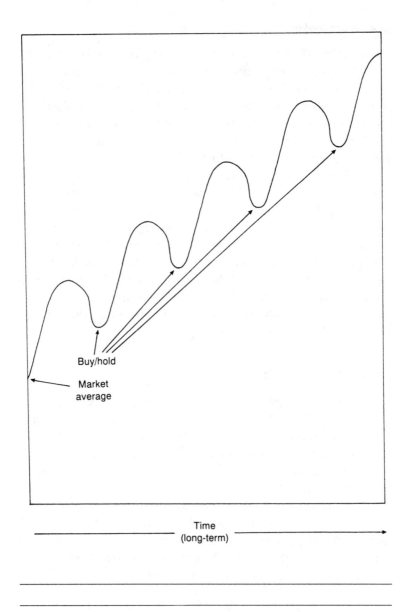

Buy/hold

Market
average

Time
(long-term)

Decision Requirements

The major decision for a new investor is to select an index or growth fund. Whether index or growth, each fund has its own characteristics. Some of the funds invest in blue chip stocks, some hold large corporations, some hold medium and small companies, some focus on new companies, some buy only those companies which have certain growth rates, etc. Your objective in selecting a fund is to insure that its investment goals are consistent with your own. A competent broker can help you find such a fund.

An experienced investor using this strategy can select either a fund or individual stocks. However, unless you have a large amount of capital with which to buy a variety of growth stocks, you should select an index or growth fund to obtain the benefits of diversification and long-term capital gains.

Strategy #2: Buy and Upgrade

General Description

The objective of the buy and upgrade strategy is to achieve long-term capital gains above those made by the market averages. To implement this strategy an investor must have enough capital to purchase a diversified portfolio of stocks. This strategy also requires the investor to review the contents of his or her portfolio to determine which stocks should be held and which sold. To use this strategy successfully, an investor must be able to time the tops and bottoms of the market cycle.

Emotion Control Requirements

This strategy requires selling some stocks when other investors are euphoric at the top of the market cycle, and it requires buy-

Figure 5–3   Strategy #2, Buy and Upgrade

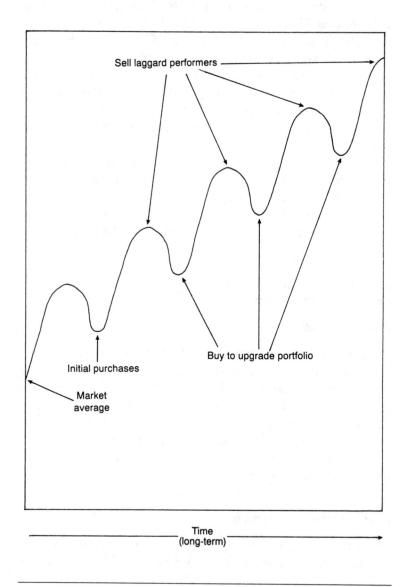

Sell laggard performers

Buy to upgrade portfolio

Initial purchases

Market
average

Time
(long-term)

ing some stocks when others are selling in panic at the bottom of the cycle. This strategy also requires the investor to control his or her fear as the market is declining through its bear phase.

Decision Requirements

Evidence of the poorer performance of some stocks will appear during the bull phase of the market cycle. (The laggards in the portfolio will advance the smallest percentages or may even decline.) The person using this strategy sells these stocks during the topping out phase of the cycle. The investor then waits for the next bottom to buy stocks that can perform better. An investor wishing assistance with stock selection can refer to the *Value Line Investment Survey,* which ranks stocks in terms of their potential for performance for the next five years.

Strategy #3: Buy and Sell

General Description

The objective of the buy and sell strategy is to achieve maximum capital gains by being fully invested during bull phases and out of the market during bear phases. The individual who can use this strategy successfully achieves the largest capital gains because purchasing power increases at each market bottom. (With the money received from selling stock at or near the top of the cycle, one can buy more stock than held previously because prices have declined.)

Emotion Control Requirements

Successful use of this strategy requires the ability to resist euphoria as stock prices rise toward the top. The individual using

Figure 5–4   Strategy #3, Buy and Sell

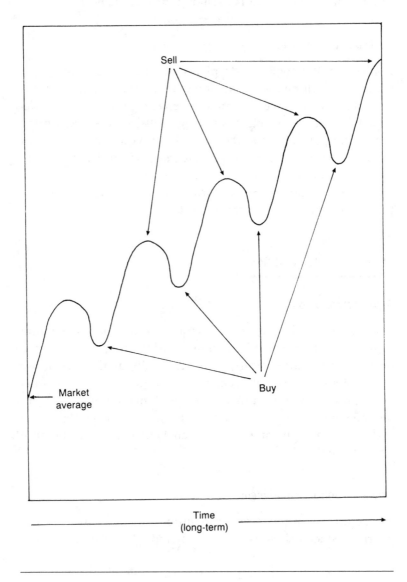

this strategy must be able to overcome this emotion and sell stocks for which a strong attachment may be felt.

This investor must also have excellent emotional independence from the crowd psychology so as to be able to sell at market tops when most others are buying, and to buy at market bottoms when most others are selling.

Decision Requirements

The successful implementation of the buy and sell strategy requires a high degree of skill at market cycle analysis. An investor should not attempt to use this strategy until he or she has been through at least two complete market cycles and has proven his or her ability to recognize market tops and bottoms as they occur.

Helpful Information

"Timing the Market Cycle" (see Appendix *Reference Information and Sources*) contains several books which can help you develop the skill to detect market cycle bottoms and tops. In addition, Chapter 6 provides illustrations of chart formations which develop at bottoms and tops in the market averages.

Note: A fourth strategy involves buying at a market bottom, selling at a top and then selling short at the top. This strategy is used by some of the most sophisticated investors who have large financial resources. However, it is too risky to recommend. (If the top of the cycle is misjudged and the market continues upward, the amount of potential loss is unlimited.)

Summaries of the three recommended strategies with their characteristics and requirements appear below. These summaries are provided to help you decide which strategy is most appropriate for you.

Strategy #1. Buy and Hold

Objective:	Long-term capital gains
Experience required:	Open to all levels
Emotion Quotient limits:	Zero to 100 percent
Emotion control requirements:	Control fear and panic as the market cycle approaches bottom. Exercise patience over the long term.
Some appropriate investments:	Index fund or growth stock fund. (If Emotion Quotient is less than 40 percent, individual growth and blue chip stocks are also appropriate investments.)
Decision requirements:	Selecting purchases to add to portfolio after each market bottom.

Strategy #2. Buy and Upgrade

Objective:	Long-term capital gains beyond those achieved by the market averages
Experience required:	In the market for at least one complete market cycle.
Emotion Quotient limits:	Zero to 40 percent

Emotion control requirements:	Resist euphoria as market approaches a top. Control fear and panic as market approaches a bottom.
Some appropriate investments:	Growth stock fund, growth stocks, blue chip stocks, stocks with low price to earnings ratios, stocks with high price appreciation potential (see Value Line Investment Survey).
Decision requirements:	Select investments to sell as market approaches a top. Select investments to buy as market completes a bottom.

Strategy #3. Buy and Sell

Objective:	Long-term capital gains above those achieved by the market averages.
Experience required:	At least two complete market cycles.
Emotion Quotient limits:	Zero to 20 percent
Emotion control requirements:	Resist euphoria as market approaches a top. Maintain complete emotional independence from the crowd. Overcome the fear-based market psychology at market bottoms, and make purchases during selling climaxes.

Some appropriate investments:

Cyclical stocks, growth stocks, blue chips, and growth and sector stock funds. Also, stocks rated highest in timeliness by *Value Line Investment Survey.*

Decision requirements:

Deciding when to buy and sell. Deciding what to purchase after the market has made a bottom.

Choosing a Strategy

The choice of a strategy is yours to make. Here is a review of the advantages and disadvantages of each.

Strategy #1

Advantages

- ◆ Requires the least amount of experience.

- ◆ Can provide large capital gains with little effort if index or equity funds are purchased.

- ◆ Investment in diversified funds involves a low level of risk.

- ◆ Commission costs are the lowest.

Disadvantages

- ◆ Potential exists for high degree of emotional stress during bear markets.

- ◆ Assets are committed for long periods, necessitating strict control of personal or family budget.

Strategy #2

Advantages

- ◆ Provides larger capital gains than Strategy #1 for an investor with above-average ability to select stocks.

- ◆ Less emotional stress than Strategy #1.

- ◆ Requires less experience and sophistication than Strategy #3.

Disadvantages

- ◆ Commission costs are higher than for Strategy #1.

- ◆ More emotional stress during bear markets than Strategy #3.

- ◆ Errors in stock selection can be costly.

Strategy #3

Advantages

- ◆ Highest potential for capital gains.

- ◆ An investor who can time the market cycle successfully is exposed to less emotional stress than with Strategies #1 or #2.

- ◆ Requires the least amount of budgetary control of personal or family expenses.

Disadvantages

- ◆ Errors in timing the market cycle can be costly.

- ◆ Errors in stock selection can be costly.

- ◆ Requires more time and effort than Strategies #1 or #2.

- ◆ Commission costs are higher than Strategies #1 or #2.

Chapter 6

Chart Patterns at Market Tops and Bottoms

Those who use any of the three strategies described in Chapter 5 will achieve maximum capital appreciation by making their initial and follow up purchases at market bottoms and any sales at market tops. It's therefore important to be able to identify market tops and bottoms as they occur.

This chapter presents chart formations by which to identify tops and bottoms. When they develop, these patterns can be seen in the chart of the Dow Jones Industrial Average (DJIA). *The Wall Street Journal* and *Investor's Daily* print and update this chart every weekday. *Barron's National Business* and *Financial Weekly* also prints this chart in its "Market Laboratory" section. Many public libraries subscribe to these newspapers.

Chart Patterns at Market Tops

The price patterns that form market tops take a variety of shapes. Note that the patterns shown in this chapter are intended as illustrations of the broad outline of each shape. They are not intended to be realistic. Actual price patterns have many more irregularities than are shown in these charts.

Mountain Top

The simplest pattern to identify is created when an uptrend changes directly into a downtrend (see Figure 6–1).

This mountain top shape reflects two distinct phases of stock market psychology. In the uptrend phase investors are convinced that the market will continue its steep rise. They are anxious to buy and bid prices up rapidly. But at some point—either because of unexpected bad news or because cash and available credit become exhausted—prices suddenly start to drop as stock holders become convinced the long rise has ended.

In the downtrend phase prices decline as rapidly as they rose, and a bear market develops. This single top chart pattern, where a bull phase advance changes directly into a bear phase decline, is the most common of the topping out formations. Within the last seventy-five years single tops in the DJIA occurred in October 1929, August 1932, March 1937, May 1946, December 1968, January 1973, October 1987, and July 1990.

Head and Shoulders Top

Another price pattern which occurs at market tops has a vague resemblance to a person's head and shoulders, so it is called a head and shoulders top (see Figure 6–2).

The head and shoulders pattern usually takes six months to a year to develop. Head and shoulders patterns come in various forms. Either shoulder can be higher than the other. There can be two shoulders on either or both sides of the head. The head can be a sharp peak as in the single top, or it can take several months to form.

Double Top

Another topping pattern is called a double top. The second top occurs at approximately the same price level as the first. After

Figure 6–1   From Uptrend to Downtrend (Single Top)

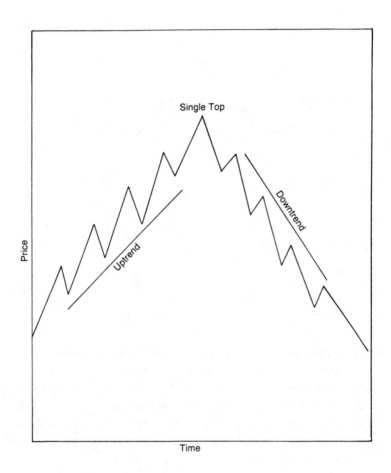

Figure 6–2   Head and Shoulders Top

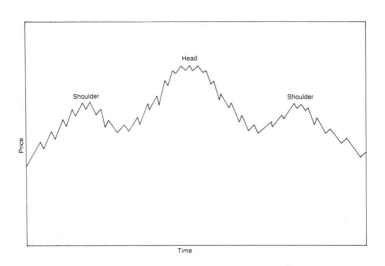

reaching the first top, the buyers make another attempt to surpass it, but fail because there are too many stockholders who
wanted to sell at the first top but didn't. After this strong, pent-
up selling pressure overcomes the weaker buying demand, the
market goes into an extended decline. Double tops can be as
close together as several weeks, or as far apart as a year or
longer (see Figure 6–3).

Figure 6–3   Double Top

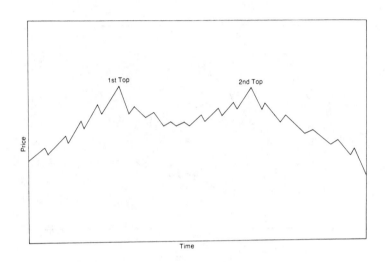

Triple Top

Closely related to the double top is the triple top. In this pattern the buyers fail twice to surpass the first top ,and the market then goes into a bear phase (see Figure 6–4). Triple tops take between several months to more than a year to form. The height of the three tops can vary slightly. They can be equidistant from each other, or the distance can vary.

Figure 6–4   Triple Top

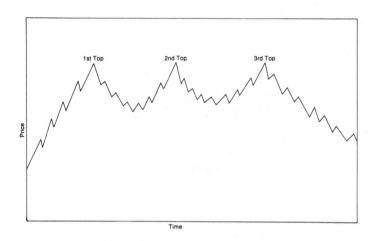

Rounding Top

Another topping pattern, which resembles an inverted saucer, is called a rounding top. This top represents a gradual switch from excess demand for stocks to excess supply as the prospects for the economy slowly change from positive to negative. Rounding tops usually develop when the market has been rising slowly. The slow uptrend converts itself into the gentle curve of the rounding top, which in turn converts to a slow downtrend. Rounding tops take several months to a year to form (see Figure 6–5).

Figure 6–5   Rounding Top

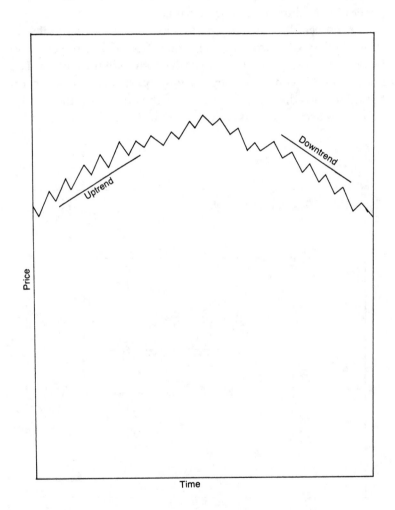

Descending Triangle

A rare top pattern, delineated by two converging straight lines, is called a descending triangle even though the third side is generally not drawn (see Figure 6–6).

A descending triangle can be envisioned as a struggle between sellers who are becoming more fearful and buyers who believe that prices are a bargain at the bottom of the pattern. The bottom line becomes a temporary support level as prices rebound toward the top side. However, the bounce off the bottom gradually becomes weaker. The fears of the sellers are eventu-

Figure 6–6   Descending Triangle

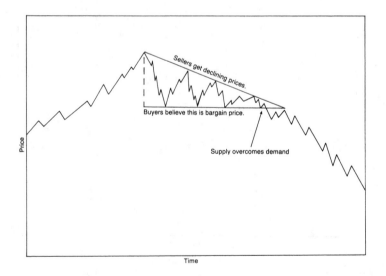

ally confirmed when the price declines through the support level.

A descending triangle signaling the top of a bull market is usually a large pattern taking several months to a year or so to complete itself. Note that smaller descending triangles of several weeks to a couple of months duration can occur during the subsequent bear market decline.

Broadening Formation

Another rare topping pattern is called a broadening formation. It is characterized by higher tops and lower bottoms, and has the appearance of a megaphone aimed at an audience on the right side of the chart (see Figure 6–7).

This formation develops as periods of increasing speculation are interspersed with periods of more determined profit taking. As it turns out, the profit takers prove to be right when the cash and credit for continuing speculation is exhausted.

Chart Patterns at Market Bottoms

The patterns formed by the DJIA at bottoms of bear markets are inversions of the patterns formed at the tops. The successful investor must learn how to recognize market bottoms because this ability provides opportunities to make purchases at low prices.

Single Bottom

One of the most common patterns formed at market cycle bottoms is the single bottom, when a downtrend is converted directly into an uptrend (see Figure 6–8).

Figure 6–7   Broadening Formation

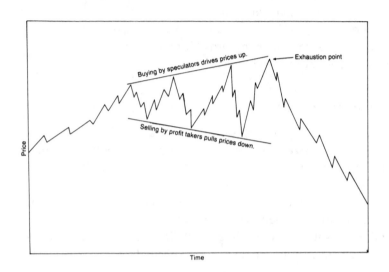

In most cases the downtrend reflects the prospects for a continuing decline in the economy. At the low point the prospects start to improve. Those buyers who can foresee the better times coming bid up prices, and an uptrend begins.

In the last sixty-five years single bottoms in the DJIA have occurred in 1932, 1938, 1943, 1949, 1957, 1962, 1966, 1969, 1982, and 1987.

Other types of bottoms occur much less frequently and reflect economic conditions which are more difficult to interpret or which change more gradually.

Figure 6–8   From Downtrend to Uptrend (Single Bottom)

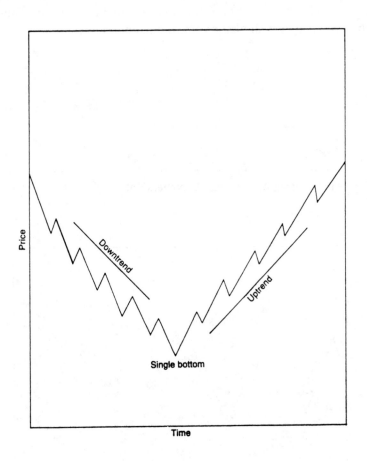

Inverted Head and Shoulders

The inverted head and shoulders pattern which follows (see Figure 6–9) has characteristics similar to those of the head and shoulders top. It takes six months to over a year to develop, there can be more than one shoulder on either or both sides, and the head can be a single bottom or a rounded formation.

Figure 6–9   Inverted Head and Shoulders Bottom

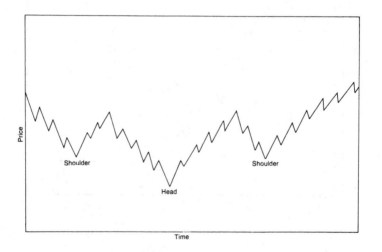

Figure 6–10   Double Bottom

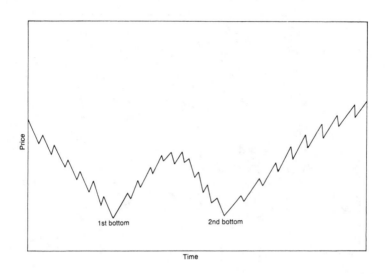

Double and Triple Bottoms

The double and triple bottom patterns which appear next (see Figures 6–10 and 6–11) reflect the uncertainties which can occur as the economy struggles to emerge from a sharp decline. The first bottom is formed as investors assume the decline will end soon. But if the economic indicators remain mixed for a while, the investment community may waver in its conviction that the worst is over. In these cases the market average declines, to test the preceding low point or points. When the average does not fall to a lower low on the second or third occasion, the test has been passed and the bull phase of the next cycle begins.

Figure 6-11 Triple Bottom

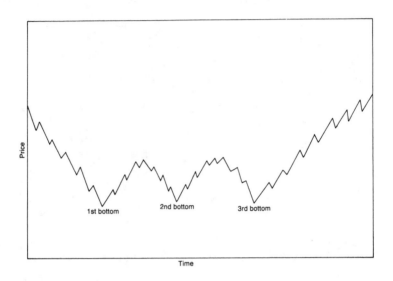

Rounded Bottoms

The rounded bottoms which appear at times reflect a gradual change in the psychology of the investment community after a prolonged economic decline. The shift in sentiment from bearish to bullish is slow and labored. The economic uncertainties persist for months before confidence is gradually restored and the uptrend finally becomes evident (see Figure 6–12).

Figure 6–12   Rounding Bottom

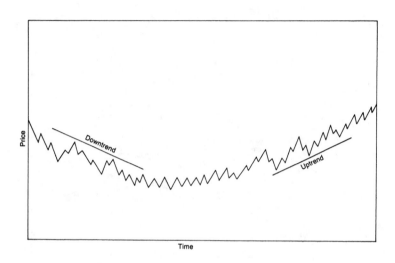

Ascending Triangle

The ascending triangle is a rare pattern, which reflects a battle between buyers and sellers (see Figure 6–13). The horizontal top line of the pattern represents the level at which many sellers are willing to sell. The large amount of stock they have for sale at this level provides a temporary barrier to further price advances. However, buyers become more and more convinced that economic conditions are improving. Their increasing eager-

Figure 6–13   Ascending Triangle

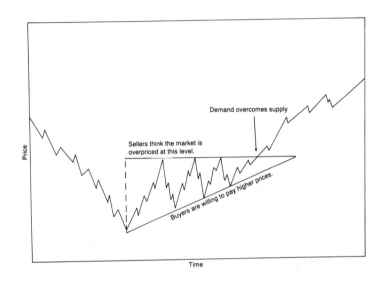

ness results in higher bottoms (represented by the rising line). Eventually the demand for stock surpasses the supply, and the resistance is broken. The stage has been set for a new bull market.

Note that smaller ascending triangles can be formed during the subsequent rise toward a bull market top.

Self-Education

As indicated above, these illustrations of patterns have been simplified to facilitate recognition. The patterns formed by actual fluctuations in the market averages are not always so obvious.

Developing the ability to interpret these patterns (which also occur in individual stocks) requires considerable self-education. After developing this ability, you will be able to implement Strategy #2, buy and upgrade, successfully. You will then be able to identify specific stocks to sell at market tops and to buy at market bottoms.

Chapter 7

Selling Near the Top

Emotional euphoria often develops as the market approaches a peak. The general public and the financial community fall in love with stock investments. Underwriters bring many new issues onto the market for distribution to eager buyers. Aggressive stock fund managers increase their stock holdings and decrease their cash reserves as the market averages continue their climb. An atmosphere of wild speculation develops as the general public catches the speculative fever and jumps onto the band wagon. It seems that few are willing to be left behind as the stock market roars off into the stratosphere.

Your interests are best served by remaining independent of the euphoric emotions at the top of a market cycle. When the stock market is soaring and most people are convinced it's a one-way street to riches, it's time to start thinking about when to sell rather than what to buy.

Strategies #2 and #3 involve making sales near the top of a bull market. The ability to sell near the top is one of the most valuable skills an investor can possess. To develop this capability, you must learn how to recognize the imminence of a top, remain aloof from the emotional hysteria, and maintain control over greed. Let's consider each of these requirements.

Recognizing a Top

As indicated in Chapter 6, topping out formations occur in a variety of patterns. When euphoria takes control of the market psychology, however, the speculative excesses that develop usually result in a single top blow-off because the amount of money and credit available to drive the market upward is exhausted. At some point there will be too little buying power to maintain the upward momentum. When the price rise stalls, profit takers start selling, which drives prices lower. Once the downtrend starts it gathers momentum quickly. Thus, if you decide to use Strategy #2 or #3, the best time to sell is while conditions still look very favorable and while prices are rising.

A point to remember is that the longer a bull market lasts, the more likely it is to end in a euphoric frenzy. This is true because the longevity of the upward trend gives the impression that it will last forever. People become accustomed to rising prices and forget they can fall too.

As a bull market matures, there are characteristic signs which warn that the end of the rise is near:

- Stock market averages have been making record highs, and these advances are reported in the headlines.

- Stock market trading volume has also been setting new records.

- Most stock market commentators predict much higher prices for the market.

- Your friends and business associates boast about how much money they're making in the market, and offer hot tips.

- The majority of economists predict more economic prosperity ahead.

◆ Low-priced stocks are rising as people with only a few dollars to risk start playing the market.

◆ The great majority of stock market advisory services are bullish.

◆ There is a speculative atmosphere at many brokerage firms, where customers assemble to watch the latest prices and pass along rumors. The opportunity to make quick profits as the market rises fast arouses excessive greed in individuals. They buy the hot stock(s) of the week, call options, new issues, penny stocks, blind pools, and other high-risk items. This type of excessive speculation sets the stage for the end of the bull phase of the market cycle.

Maintaining Emotional Independence

The ability to think in a contrary fashion is especially valuable as the top of a market approaches. Here are some questions to ask yourself to avoid the euphoria that dominates the crowd at bull market tops.

◆ Are you beginning to feel that stock prices can keep rising forever? (Remember that bull markets don't usually last more than a few years.)

◆ Are you reluctant to take large paper profits because of the tax consequences? (Paying taxes on capital gains is the unpleasant part of being successful in the market.)

◆ Do you believe your stocks can maintain their price levels while all others fall? (The chance of this happening is small.)

♦ Are you feeling competitive? Are you comparing your paper profits to those of your friends and associates? If so, consider this. If everyone you know in the market has large paper profits, it follows that buying demand must be close to a peak. (That's the time to prepare to sell if you are using Strategy #3.)

Controlling Greed

When euphoria dominates the psychology of investors and speculators, it becomes more difficult to keep greed under control. Here are some thoughts and suggestions to help you in this effort.

♦ It's not necessary to sell out at the highest price to be a successful investor. The few people who sell at the highest price do so by virtue of sheer luck—not skill.

♦ Because so many stocks are making big gains near the top of a bull market, your broker may have suggestions of other stocks to switch into. In making such recommendations, the broker will be appealing to your greed. It's best to decline the invitation, since the broker's motivation may be the bigger commissions that would be earned as you make more trades. Don't let the broker's greed unleash yours.

♦ Your broker may try to convince you to open a margin account to increase your leverage. This is another appeal to your greed. This invitation should also be declined.

♦ Financial broadcasters on television recommend many stocks as a bull market approaches its top. It would be unwise to follow up on these suggestions. Once a recommendation has been broadcast, the price of the stock reflects this publicity. If you buy the stock afterward, you will pay a premium price along with all others who follow that advice. (What is known to everyone is not worth much.)

Selling Individual Stocks

Strategy #2, buy and upgrade, calls for selecting your worst performing stocks and selling them near the top of the market cycle. However, at each market top some stocks top out early, some top out with the market cycle, and some top out late. If you select two or more stocks to sell, you would want to sell each one near its own top.

A procedure for achieving this objective involves several steps.

1. As the bull market matures, visit your broker's office or your library and examine the charts for each of the stocks you plan to sell. (Several visits may be necessary.) Or you may choose to subscribe to one of the stock charting services listed in the *References and Information* Appendix.

2. As you review the charts, look for topping patterns similar to those that appear in Chapter 6.

3. Sell each stock as it completes its own topping pattern.

Selling Out a Portfolio

Strategy #3, buy and sell, calls for selling out your entire portfolio near the top of the market cycle. You should sell all your stocks when you observe the excessive speculation which leads to a blow-off single top.

However, if excessive speculation and euphoria are not evident, and the market is making a long, extended topping formation such as a rounding top, you can use the same sales procedure as that outlined for Strategy #2.

Developing the ability to determine which phase the market cycle is in requires extensive study. You will find such study materials in the section of the *Reference and Information Sources* Appendix titled, "Timing the Market."

These sources provide information and present analytic techniques to detect market bottoms and tops. Those techniques will help you to time purchases and sales to maximize your capital gains over the long run.

Chapter 8

When the Bubble Bursts

The seeds for the collapse of each bull market are sewn in advance. A few astute investors sense correctly that the market is dangerously overpriced, and sell out just before the bubble bursts. But the great majority of investors are caught by surprise, and watch the value of their investments decline rapidly.

In general, bull markets are killed by excessive speculation by the private sector, or by fiscal mismanagement by the government. Here's a list of the bull markets which ended in speculative blow-offs followed by selling panics. The list provides a perspective on the causes, frequency, and character of market panics.

Table 8–1   Thumbnail Sketches of Market Panics

1837 Excessive credit fueled too much speculation in purchases of commodities, manufacturing companies, and western real estate. When prices reached excessive heights, the speculative bubble burst. A selling panic followed.

1853 Excessive speculation fueled by liberal bank loans drove prices up too high. Selling of American securities on a

---

large scale began in London. Banks called in their loans to speculators and the market crashed.

1857 Excessive credit fueled speculation in mines and railroads. Uncontrolled inflation caused the economy and the stock market to collapse.

1873 United States and British bankers lent too much money to railroads, farmers, and stock brokers. Brokers lent money to speculators at 5 to 10 percent margin rates. Speculation in the stock market was rampant. When the economy stopped expanding, the banking system collapsed, and the stock market crashed.

1884 Many brokerage houses and banks went under because of credit manipulation and speculative schemes.

1893 The federal government printed too much money. Inflation was rampant. There was wild speculation in railroad and industrial stocks. Foreigners purchased gold from our treasury and drained it until our citizens lost confidence in U.S. currency. Hundreds of banks failed.

1901 A bear market decline became a free fall when margin calls by the brokerage houses caused massive liquidation of accounts.

1907 Several years of rapid inflation and excessive speculation came to an abrupt end when big operators in the stock market sold out their positions at the top. Overextended credit and insufficient reserves precipitated a run on the banks; hundreds failed.

1913 Fear of impending World War I caused a collapse in stock and commodity prices. European investors sold American securities to raise cash to buy gold as a safe haven. Many bank failures resulted from speculating in the market. The

New York Stock Exchange was forced to close for several months.

1921 Excessive expansion of money and credit after World War I caused runaway inflation and a subsequent collapse of the economy.

1929 Excessive credit, purchases on low margins, and wild public speculation in the stock market resulted in sky-rocketing prices which could not be sustained. Margin calls accelerated the decline.

1937 The Federal Reserve Board pursued a tight money policy until corporate profits were decimated and the stock market collapsed.

1962 The Federal Reserve Board restricted credit tightly to counter an acceleration in inflation. Anticipating a recession, the stock market fell rapidly.

1974 The Arab oil embargo hampered our economy and caused panic selling in the stock market.

1987 Merger mania and leveraged buyouts fueled by junk bonds resulted in excessive speculation. When the bubble burst, program trading and margin calls accelerated the decline.

Dealing with Bear Markets

Since bull markets don't last forever, the investor in the market for the long-run needs a strategy for handling the ensuing bear market. Each of the three strategies described earlier help the investor deal with this problem. While the three strategies differ in terms of their requirements for timing and selection decisions, they all contain the premise that market bottoms and selling climaxes provide the best buying opportunities. Hopefully, you will have the fortitude to buy in those situations. Indeed, making purchases during a selling climax, while panic reigns, is an extreme test of courage.

Buying During a Selling Climax

Assuming you will have the courage, you will be able to act on the fact that the shares of many equity funds will be available at bargain prices. Here are some alternative purchases to consider:

◆ A selling climax gives you a rare opportunity to buy blue chip stocks at a discount.

◆ Growth companies with high profit margins will be available at lower price/earning ratios than usual.

◆ Some companies run by conservative managers prefer to operate without any debt. These companies are in a relatively better position to survive through difficult times.

◆ Some volatile stocks will proportionately decline much further during a selling climax. They will be available at rare bargain prices. However, their volatility does signify an extra element of risk. Such stocks should not comprise more than a small fraction of your portfolio.

Resisting Personal Panic

When a selling climax develops, each person must deal with the contagious quality of the mass panic which accompanies this activity. How can you resist the emotions inherent in the situation? How do you keep your cool while others are so fearful?

Each individual must find his or her answer to these questions. Perhaps the following suggestions can help you develop your solution to the problem.

1. If you enjoy discussing the market with your friends and associates, do so without revealing your own purchases and sales. For example, if your friend doesn't know you have stock in the ABC company, he won't feel obliged to offer his advice to sell it during a panic. Or perhaps a business associate has sold her shares in the XYZ corporation during a panic situation, and you've decided to buy some. If you told her of your intention, you shouldn't be surprised to see a strong negative reaction from her at the revelation. Nor would it be surprising if one of your well-intentioned friends let you know he thought you had lost your sanity if you have revealed your plans to buy anything when the consensus is that a financial disaster is imminent.

2. Another way to stay calm during panics is to shun investments which leave you vulnerable to unnecessary risks.

   There are blue chip stocks which maintain their dividends through good times and bad. Widely diversified mutual stock funds provide more protection against paper losses than sector funds do. Some companies with small market share and others with excessive debt go bankrupt or out of business during recessions and should be avoided.

3. Leaving your stock certificates in the broker's custody also introduces an unnecessary element of risk. The conditions that result in a market panic threaten the viability of some brokerage firms. The Securities Investor Protection Corporation (SIPC) has reported the failure of between five and ten brokerage firms each

year for the last decade. If this happens to your firm, any certificates you have on deposit with them may be unavailable to you for several months, while the SIPC straightens out the situation and arranges for the distribution of the firm's remaining assets.

To eliminate that problem, instruct your broker to send your certificates to you. (You must maintain a cash account and have paid for the stocks before the broker will do this.)

4. When economic disasters occur, they generate much publicity. The media thrive on bad news. Television reporters and commentators dwell on each aspect of the problem and analyze it thoroughly. As an individual exposed to this gloom and doom, you should try to preserve a balanced perspective. Don't allow yourself to be panicked by the media. Here are some points to remember which can help in this regard.

Broadcasters emphasize the frightening aspects of the situation to hold the attention of the viewer. It is not in your interest to be intimidated. One of their standard techniques is to call in experts to make predictions about how bad things will become.

As a viewer you can control your inclination to panic by recognizing there are no experts when it comes to predicting the future. They're just guessing and there's no reason to base your stock market decisions on their guesses.

The end of the world and other dire forecasts have been made many times. Those who let themselves be panicked by such doomsday prognosticators live to regret it.

5. The most unnerving thing about selling panics are the uncertainties which accompany them. How low will stock prices go before they recover? Will the recession be deep or shallow? Will it be short or long? will a recession develop into a depression? Will your bank fail? Will your broker to out of business? And the big question, will this be the end of Western Civilization as we know it? (This last question was raised and answered, "Yes!" by some commentators during the selling panic of October, 1987.)

To deal with a market panic, you may wish to take some action to maintain your peace of mind. An investment which has done this for some people is the ownership of shares in gold mining companies. The disasters which send the market down usually result in higher prices for gold as people buy it for safe haven or for protection against inflation or other calamities. If you use Strategy #1 or #2, buying some shares in a gold mining company can insulate you from a personal panic reaction.

If you decide to purchase shares in the gold mining industry, it's important to choose the company carefully. Here are some criteria by which to make your selection. Look for a company that:

- is currently making a good profit from the sale of its gold production

- has a relatively low cost per ounce of gold refined

- has enough proven gold ore reserves to support a steady production flow for at least 10 years

- has an active program to discover new deposits of gold or acquire producing gold mines from other companies.

This information is available from the *Value Line Investment Survey* and from *Standard and Poor's Stock Reports.* Holding shares in gold mining companies to comprise between 10 and 15 percent of your portfolio can provide you with a personal emotional buffer against selling panics.

Chapter 9

 # Investors' Relationships with Brokers

Developing a Long-Term Relationship

As indicated earlier, a long-term approach to the market is more likely to produce significant profits. And a long-term relationship with one competent broker is likely to be more profitable than switching around from one to another. It takes time to develop a good working partnership. One of your major objectives should be to establish and maintain one.

The reason some people switch from one broker to another is that negative feelings arise between them and their brokers. Let's review the causes of such negative feelings, to help you avoid the potential problem areas.

Communicating with Your Broker

Provide Information About Yourself

One cause of problems is poor communication. It's the broker's responsibility to know the customer. He or she should ask about your investment objectives, your ability to take risks, and your previous experiences in the market.

For your part, you should reveal appropriate information about yourself. (Ask for assurance that all personal information will be kept confidential.) If you are new to the market, let the broker know, and request that he or she not push you into transactions. If you are eager to get recommendations, indicate that. If you've had emotional reactions to market movements, which resulted in losses, provide a description of those investment experiences.

Also describe problems you had with any previous brokers. Did he or she recommend more losers than winners? Did the broker advise against an investment or trade which turned out well? Did the broker appear to be more interested in commissions than in your success?

By being up front about past problems, you warn the broker of potential sore points. The broker who listens to your descriptions of previous difficulties will be aware of your concerns and will be more likely to avoid making you uncomfortable by treating you inappropriately.

Ask Questions About Stock Recommendations

If your broker calls to recommend a stock you know nothing about, it's appropriate for you to ask some questions before deciding whether to follow a suggestion. One of the most important items to learn is if the firm underwrote this stock or is a member of the syndicate distributing it. If so, the broker probably has a quota of shares to sell. If this is the situation, you must be certain that buying this stock is in line with your objectives and your tolerance for risk. Here are some additional questions to ask about any stock with which you are unfamiliar.

- ◆ What industry is the company in? Is this industry new? Is it established and growing? Is it cyclical? Has it matured? Investments in new industries carry the most potential for reward but are also the riskiest. Investments in established, growth industries provide the best opportunities for capital appreciation in the long run. Investments in cyclical industries fluctuate the most, so it's critical to buy them near the bottom of a cycle instead of close to the top. Investments in mature industries usually provide better than average dividends, but lower than average capital appreciation.

◆ Is the company making a profit? If yes, what is the price/earnings ratio? The price/earnings ratio is a yardstick for evaluating the earnings power of a corporation. By comparing the price/earnings ratio of companies in the same industry, you obtain an idea of which companies are more profitable. Companies with lower price/earnings ratios are more profitable than those with higher ratios. If the company is losing money, you should ask the broker why he or she believes the company can become profitable. You should also recognize that unprofitable companies are riskier than profitable ones.

◆ Where does the company stand in its industry? Is it one of the largest, medium sized, or one of the smallest? Companies with the largest market share in an industry usually have the best chance of surviving and remaining profitable. Companies with the smallest market share are more likely to fail or to be unable to compete effectively.

◆ Why does the broker believe the price will rise? When you hear the reasons, make a note of them. Then, whether you buy the stock or not, as events develop, you'll be able to evaluate the validity of the broker's reasoning.

Avoid making a decision while on the phone. Ask for additional information such as a Standard and Poor's yellow sheet, a prospectus, or a Form 10K report. After reviewing this type of information, you may want to do some further investigation on your own before deciding whether to buy.

Asking these questions and requesting such information will let the broker know you intend to evaluate each recommendation and he or she will learn that you don't intend to be rushed into any decision. This is important because if you buy under pressure, you'll be more inclined to develop negative feelings if the price of the stock goes down instead of up.

Provide Guidelines to the Broker

It's in the client's interest to make relevant information available to the broker so that recommendations can be appropriate. The customer should also tell the broker if help in selecting stocks is needed, and if so, which types of stocks are appropriate. (If you prefer the blue chips, you won't be comfortable with a broker who recommends stocks you never heard of. On the other hand, if you're excited by the potential, and can handle the risks of investing in growth companies, the blue chips may be too conservative for you.)

Let the broker know if you want any restrictions on the interactions between you.

- ◆ If you don't want to be annoyed by calls on the job, let the broker know.

- ◆ Tell your broker if you prefer particular categories of investments such as:

  Index funds

  Growth stock funds

  Blue chip or growth stocks

  Stocks priced between $5 and $15 (or higher ranges)

Companies with no debt or very low debt to equity ratios

Stocks with low price/earnings ratios

Giving guidelines like these will help insure you will only be called in regard to something relevant to your interests.

◆ Give the broker a general idea of how often you would like to be called: frequently, once in a while, or only when he has found a stock which meets your criteria.

◆ Let the broker know if you want to receive research reports if the firm publishes them. If you do, remember that by the time you receive the report, the price of the stock will probably reflect any information in it because of others who have seen it and have decided to buy or sell.

◆ If you have a demanding job and a busy social life and won't be able to return phone calls quickly, let the broker know.

◆ If there is any other restriction on the relationship you feel is necessary, stating it will help insure the partnership will be one in which you can be comfortable for the long run.

Dependence Leads to Problems

Customers' relationships with stock brokers vary from total dependence to total independence. Following are descriptions of five different types of relationships along this continuum.

1. A customer willing to let the broker make all decisions opens what is called a discretionary account. He or she

becomes totally dependent on the broker's judgment. By signing a discretionary agreement, the client gives the broker advance approval to make purchases and sales for the account. The broker is supposed to learn about the client's objectives, tolerance for risk, etc., and make only those investments which are suitable. However, it doesn't always work that way.

Every year some brokers violate SEC regulations and abuse the fiduciary relationships with their clients. People who sign discretionary agreements with incompetent or unethical brokers take unnecessary risks. Because of the problems which can occur in this type of account, the prospects for a good long-term relationship are small. Some discontented customers have to pursue arbitration or take legal action to rectify the mistreatment they receive.

2. Some people don't want to relinquish control completely by opening a discretionary account. But they don't feel capable of generating their own investment ideas. They believe the broker will select investments to meet their objectives and they open either a margin or a cash account.

In this type of relationship the customer retains control but is still dependent upon the competence and moral code of the broker. Some brokers use high-pressure sales techniques, appeals to greed, misrepresentation, or outrageous promises to convince the client to follow their advice.

These abuses usually occur because the client lets the broker dominate the relationship. He or she assumes the broker knows more about the market and will select appropriate investments. But the primary motivation of some brokers is to generate commissions—not to make profits for the client.

3. Some better-informed customers establish a relationship based on equality with the broker. Both the customer and the broker generate ideas and then evaluate them jointly to determine which are better suited to meet the client's goals and are within her or his tolerance for risk.

    The broker does not try to sell the ideas but acts as a source of information and provides the customer with relevant research materials if they are available from the firm. The broker strives to gain the client's trust by providing accurate information and competent advice, and by behaving in an ethical manner.

    This type of customer asks for relevant information (see list of questions presented above) so that appropriate action can be taken. The customer thus maintains control of the account and reserves the right to make the final decisions. With good faith efforts from both parties, this type of relationship is conducive to a long-term association.

4. Other investors, who are confident of their ability to select investments, establish a semi-independent relationship. They limit the broker's role to that of providing the information or research materials relevant to their investment interests. They rarely request the broker's advice.

    Some brokers are willing to accept this type of service oriented role. These brokers know sophisticated clients are easier to deal with because they have made the effort to educate themselves about investments. They make few requests for information and don't take much of the broker's time. When the client knows what she or he wants, the relationship is more durable over the long run.

5. In a relationship wherein the customer is totally independent, interaction and communication requirements are minimal. The customer generates all investment ideas and does not request advice from the broker— just information. The client retains control over all transactions in the account. The broker is expected to take orders and execute them efficiently.

This type of customer does the research and stock selection and accepts full responsibility for decisions. Because the broker's role is so limited, there are usually few problems in this type of relationship.

Table 9–1 summarizes these relationships. The chart also shows the connection between customer dependency and the potential for anger at the broker. The primary reason for a customer's anger is declining asset value in the account when his or her perception is that the decline was caused by the broker's incompetence or unethical behavior.

Unethical Brokers

Brokers who are hungry for commissions use sales tactics which foster negative reactions from their customers. The Securities Exchange Commission (SEC) is responsible for overseeing problems between clients and their brokers. Statistics maintained by the SEC Office of Consumer Affairs indicate that more than 15,000 complaints against brokers are filed annually. The following section describes some broker actions which make customers feel abused and angry enough to make complaints.

Table 9–1   Investors' Relationships to Brokers

Total Dependence	Semi-Dependence	Equality	Semi-Independence	Total Independence
Client's discretionary account allows broker to make transactions without the client's knowledge. (Blanket approval has been given in advance.) Some unethical brokers churn the account and violate other SEC regulations. These abuses result in short-lived relationships.	Broker sells investment ideas to client with cash or margin account. Some brokers use high pressure, deception and/or appeals to greed or other emotions. These aggressive brokers dominate the client and generate commissions for themselves rather than profits for the client. This one-sidedness is not conducive to a long-term relationship.	Client and broker generate ideas and assess their suitability for client. Client insists on being well informed before making decisions. Broker does not seek to dominate the client and earns trust by giving accurate information and competent advice. This cooperation facilitates development of a long-term relationship.	Client generates most ideas and insures suitability and good fit with objectives. Client selects investments to investigate. Client requests information and research reports, rarely asks for advice and makes all investment decisions. These conditions favor a beneficial long-term relationship.	Client generates all ideas, makes all investment decisions and accepts total responsibility for profits and losses. Broker's role is limited to giving information and executing orders. As long as the broker provides these services efficiently, there is no difficulty in maintaining a good long-term relationship.

High Potential for Anger at Broker   ←   Diminishing Potential for Anger   →   Low Potential for Anger at Broker

Account Churning

A broker who makes excessive trades in a client's account to generate commissions is said to be churning the account. This activity is most likely to occur when the customer has relinquished control over the account to a discretionary account manager or to a dominating, unethical broker. If excessive commissions are extracted from an account, the total value of the account often declines over a period of time.

When a customer believes the account has been churned, he or she may seek arbitration or file a civil suit to recover damages. Account churning not only results in the loss of capital but in a loss of opportunity and time, and in aggravation to the client.

Unauthorized Trading

Some brokers make trades in margin or cash accounts without the client's verbal or written approval. (If a customer has not signed a discretionary account agreement, it is standard practice to give orders to the broker verbally.) But some brokers make unauthorized trades for a customer and believe they are acting in the client's best interest.

For example, a customer may have told the broker she or he had an interest in a particular stock. If the stock started going up and the broker could not reach the client, the broker might decide to buy the stock. However, since the client did not give explicit approval for that transaction, the broker would have made an unauthorized trade. Any customer who had not signed a discretionary account agreement would have good reason to be angry at the broker for that action. (Since sudden reversals are common in the stock market, the broker could have done more harm than good.)

A customer who wishes to avoid this problem must establish himself or herself as the only one to make the decisions for the account. When the broker knows the customer wants to retain control over all transactions, there is little possibility the broker will take any well-intended but unjustifiable action.

Misrepresentation

In their efforts to convince a customer to purchase a stock, some brokers make statements that are misleading, exaggerated, or untrue. For example, a broker may mislead a customer by claiming receipt of information from a reliable source, when in fact it was just a rumor. The broker may also exaggerate, by stating a company's earning will double next year when there is little or no basis for predicting such an increase. Or the broker may say a company will receive a large contract, when the company has only entered a bid and has no assurance of getting the contract.

Misrepresentations such as these might be taken at face value by a gullible customer who may authorize a purchase. If the broker's claim turns out to be unjustified, the value of the customer's account may decline. People who take the initiative in generating their own investment ideas are not vulnerable to misrepresentation or duplicity by this type of action.

Unsuitability

When a broker makes purchase recommendations, it's his or her responsibility to insure the suggestions are suitable for that customer. For example, if a customer's objectives are preservation of capital and current income, the broker should select a fund or a stock which meets those goals. If a customer is seeking long-term capital gains, the broker should recommend a growth fund or a stock with good potential for price appreciation. A stock with volatile price action might be suitable for a successful businessperson, but the volatility might only serve to give restless nights to a person on a low, fixed income.

The broker who recommends unsuitable stocks can arouse the customer's anxieties. On the other hand, well-informed clients who select their own stocks can choose those which are consistent with their objectives. The investor who is dependent on the broker's judgment is vulnerable both financially and emotionally. It's difficult to stay calm and rational when you lose money because of someone else's recommendations.

Taking Control

In contrast, when the customer is in the dominant role and makes the decisions, the potential for abuses by the broker diminishes. Here's an approach for establishing this type of relationship with your broker.

First, find a broker who does not seek the dominant role in the relationship. Fortunately, there are some brokers who can accept a limited role. To find such a broker and establish a long-term partnership, you should deal with the issue up front. Tell the broker you reserve the right to make the decision on each purchase and sale. Tell him or her what your investment objectives are and insist that any suggestion made be suitable for achieving those goals. Describe your risk tolerance level so that recommendations are within your comfort zone.

Second, pursue a program of self-education. Long-term success in the market is directly related to the ability to select good stocks and make timely purchases and sales. If financial success is important to you, devoting some time and effort to this endeavor must be a high-priority item. The more you increase your knowledge of the market, the easier it will be to establish a healthy relationship with your broker.

Interim Actions

Depending on your current level of knowledge about the stock market, your self-education program may take less than a year, or as much as several years. In the meantime, here are some suggestions for action with reference to the type of account you may now have: discretionary, margin, or standard cash account.

Discretionary Accounts

If you now have a discretionary account and are dissatisfied with the broker's behavior or achievement, here are some corrective actions to consider.

♦ Close the account and open a new discretionary account in another brokerage firm. Be certain the new broker has a successful record of account management by asking for and checking references. Indicate your requirements by describing your investment objectives, your tolerance for risk, and your need to be kept informed as to investments made on your behalf. If you have specific objections to actions taken by the previous broker, let the new one know that you will not tolerate such actions. Inform the broker that you intend to monitor the account transactions closely.

♦ Close the discretionary account and open a standard cash account with another broker. This will give you the opportunity to be as active in managing the account as you wish. Refer to Table 9–1. I recommend you adopt the relationship described in the center box or one of the two on the right-hand side of the chart. Choose the one that is most comfortable on the basis of your current knowledge and level of self-confidence. By selecting one of those three relationships, you'll establish that you wish to be at least an equal partner.

◆ Close the discretionary account and switch into an equity fund with a good track record through at least a complete market cycle. Select a fund whose objectives are consistent with yours.

◆ If the market is in the bear phase of its cycle, you can put your capital into a money market fund exempt from federal taxes. Select one whose assets are invested in federally insured instruments. This will protect your capital and provide a return on your investment while you wait out the bear market and pursue your self-education.

After the market makes a bottom you can reenter it and open a cash account which you can manage yourself or enlist the services of a cooperative broker.

Margin Accounts

If you are unhappy with the results of trading in a margin account, here are some alternatives to consider.

◆ Convert to a standard cash account. This will prevent you from taking high-risk actions such as borrowing too much or making uncovered short sales.

◆ Close out the account and purchase shares in an equity fund with objectives consistent with your own. This will provide the relative safety of diversification.

◆ If the market is in a bear phase, close out the account and open a cash account after the market has made a bottom.

Cash Accounts

If you now have a cash account and are satisfied with your relationship with the broker and with the results you are achieving, you should keep it.

However, if the broker insists on dominating the relationship, uses high pressure sales tactics, unethical practices, or produces poor results, you should consider some alternatives.

◆ Close out the account and find another broker with whom to make a fresh start. Let the new broker know you wish to be an equal partner in the relationship.

◆ Close out the account and buy shares in an equity fund whose objectives are consistent with yours.

◆ If the market is in a bear phase, close out the account and wait for the next market cycle bottom. In the meantime, pursue a program of self-education to improve your ability to select stocks. This will give you the self-confidence to establish a non-dependent relationship with your next broker.

Finding an Ethical Broker

The overwhelming majority of brokers are ethical. The amount of publicity unethical brokers have received in past years is out of proportion to their numbers. They live high-risk lives and when caught are often fined, imprisoned, or banned from the brokerage business.

When selecting a new broker, you should make an effort to check out his or her conformance to ethical standards. This can be done in the following manner. First, call the National Association of Securities Dealers at 1-800-289-9999 and request background information on the broker in question. If his or her record is clean, you will be given the information over the phone. However, if there is a conviction recorded against the broker, the NASD will send a written report. Rather than wait for the report, which may take a while to arrive, you may wish to contact your own state regulator, who can give you the information over the phone. You may obtain the phone number of your state regulator by calling the North American Securities Administrators Association at 1-202-737-0900.

By exercising this type of vigilance, you should be able to find an ethical broker, and form a mutually beneficial partnership.

Chapter 10

The Broker's Point of View

In Chapter 9 the value of a long-term association with a broker was stressed. However, a stable relationship can only be developed if both parties are satisfied. As a client you need a broker who is trustworthy, competent, and provides good service. Brokers also have preferences which enable them to establish and maintain a long-term relationship with a client. Brokers prefer clients who

- ◆ accept responsibility for their own decisions

- ◆ are considerate of the broker's time

- ◆ understand and conform to agreements they sign

- ◆ provide the broker with enough personal information to allow him or her to service the account effectively

On the other hand, brokers are not eager to establish relationships with clients who

- ◆ harass them verbally for events beyond their control

- ◆ press the broker to violate SEC or brokerage firm regulation

- insist on more service than the size of the account warrants

- overestimate their tolerance for risk

- try to avoid financial responsibility for their trading activities

- are disloyal in placing orders

Let's review these items and other aspects of the client/broker relationship from the broker's point of view.

Visiting the Office

Some customers open their account over the phone,call in their orders, call for quotes, send their checks in the mail—and never meet their broker face to face. As a good business practice, it makes sense for the client to visit the office and meet the broker and the branch manager. This visit provides an opportunity to put the relationship on a personal, friendly basis. If you wish to know how a brokerage office functions, the broker or the manager can explain the operation first hand and answer any questions.

Stock brokers send out monthly account statements to each client. Brokers receive many phone calls about items in the statements which customers don't understand. During a visit to the office, the broker and the customer can make a detailed review of any aspect of the statement which may be confusing to the client. This interaction can reduce or eliminate misunderstanding the monthly account statements.

If you have never been to your broker's office, make an appointment to go there. Use the meeting to develop rapport, to have your questions answered, and to establish the basis for a good relationship.

Requests for Excessive Service

In general, a broker is eager to give stock price quotes, company-related information, and research reports in anticipation of receiving an order. When you place an order, it should be executed efficiently. If there is an error in your account, it should be checked out and corrected quickly. If there's something you don't understand in your account statement, it should be explained to your satisfaction.

Beyond these basic services, the willingness of the broker to expend time and effort on your behalf will probably be proportional to the volume of business generated in your account. To obtain an idea of the relative size of your account, ask the secretary if yours is one of the smallest, medium sized, or largest. One clue you may be requesting too much service is if the secretary puts you on hold and the broker takes a long time to answer each time you call.

On the other hand, if you feel strongly that your broker is not giving you enough attention, you can either request your account be reassigned to a broker who has fewer accounts, or you can switch to another office.

Unrealistic Expectations

Some people have unrealistic expectations about what their brokers should be able to do. There are few, if any, brokers who can pick all winners. Most brokers can select more winners than losers. (If they can't, they won't be in the business for long.) If an individual depends on the broker to select stocks or give advice, he or she must expect the broker to recommend some stocks that don't perform well.

Some investors expect the broker to buy at the bottom eighth for the day and sell at the top eighth. This is unrealistic since brokers are not clairvoyant. If you have such demands and express them to the broker, you will become an annoyance.

If the broker-recommended investments in your account appreciate between 10 and 15 percent yearly, that's good performance. If they appreciate faster, you are fortunate to have such an excellent broker. If they appreciate slower, and your broker is responsible for too many losing transactions, look for a more competent broker.

Delinquencies

Brokerage firms have regulations governing the trading of stocks. One rule is that purchases must be paid for within five business days. Similarly, each sale of stock must be followed by delivery of the certificate within five business days. If the buyer and the seller each deliver in accordance with their obligation, a stock certificate is exchanged for a check on the fifth day (the settlement date). That's the way it should work.

However, if the check is not received on time from the buyer, or the stock certificate is not received on time from the seller, the broker must do extra work to resolve the problem. He or she must contact the delinquent party to obtain the delivery of the check or the certificate. And the broker must also deal with the disappointed party who has not received a check (the seller), or a certificate (the buyer). This is unpleasant work for the broker. A customer who is delinquent too often will have his or her account closed by the broker.

To establish and maintain a long-term relationship with your broker, be sure to make payments and certificate deliveries on time.

Lack of Loyalty

Some people deal with two brokerage firms—usually one full service and one discount commission house. Some individuals take advantage of the difference in commissions. After receiving a recommendation from their full-service broker, they place the order with the discount house. This abusive practice is reprehensible. It's only fair to give any order to the broker from whom you received the recommendation. Orders for which you generate the idea yourself are appropriately given to a discount commission broker.

Wasting the Broker's Time

Some anxious individuals call their broker every day just to obtain price quotes on their stocks. This is a waste of the broker's time. Anyone who wants to follow the price changes in stocks can check the business section of the daily newspaper.

Many competent, established brokers have hundreds of active accounts. The two busiest periods for a broker are the few minutes just after the market opens and the minutes before it closes. At the opening he or she will be watching to see in which direction the market and certain stocks are moving. Just prior to the close your broker will be in a hurry to place any orders before the trading stops.

If you have a busy broker, call during the slow periods of the business day unless you have an order for execution. Don't call frequently just to receive price quotes. Avoid long discussions during regular business hours unless you have an urgent matter to resolve.

Tracking Down Rumors

On any day there may be rumors about one or more companies. As a rumor is passed along by word of mouth, the content often changes. While a few rumors correctly predict an actual event, most are exaggerated, inaccurate, or completely unsubstantiated.

Some individuals ask their brokers to verify the truth of rumors. Since it's virtually impossible for the average broker to trace back a rumor to its source or otherwise verify it, the broker will not take kindly to such requests. The best way to deal with rumors is to ignore them. That way you won't be tempted to churn your own account.

Monday Morning Quarterbacking

Some customers critique the broker's performance every week. They review the weekly stock reports in the Sunday newspaper and call their broker on Monday morning. They annoy her or him with questions like these:

"My stock went down three points last week. Why didn't you tell me to get out?"

"ABC Corporation went up two points on Friday. How come you didn't tell me to buy before the move?"

"You told me to take my profit in XYZ Corporation two months ago. Now it's up another six points. Why did you get me out?"

The answer to such questions is that the broker can't see into the future. The customer who harasses the broker in this manner has little possibility of developing a long-term relationship. If you ask for and follow a broker's advice, you must accept that the broker will make a mistake now and then.

Seeking Inside Information

Trading on the basis of inside information is illegal. Neverthe-
less, some customers try to obtain inside information from their
brokers. A request for this type of information puts a broker in
an awkward position. To pass along inside information to a
customer is a violation of SEC regulations; the broker who does
this risks his or her job. If a broker gives you inside information
and you trade on the basis of that knowledge, you can be subject
to penalties. The safe course of action to follow regarding inside
information is to neither seek it nor accept it.

Margin Account Problems

Margin accounts are attractive to some individuals because of
the leverage they provide. But some customers are unaware that
interest will be charged to the account on a daily basis. They are
also surprised when the stock goes down and they receive a
margin call for more money or collateral. A margin account
client who is aware of his or her financial responsibilities is in a
better position to maintain a smooth relationship with the broker.

Tolerance for Risk

One of the important factors in determining a person's approach
to the stock market is tolerance for risk. Some people overestimate their risk tolerance. This occurs primarily with inexperienced investors. Individuals who overestimate their tolerance
for risk can become a nuisance to a broker. If they buy stocks
which start going down, they wonder if they did the right thing.

If they buy stocks which have high volatility, watching the price jump up and down makes them nervous.

Their discomfort with these situations may lead them to call the broker every day to seek reassurance. Some brokers feel imposed upon when required to deal frequently with clients who become worried or nervous about their investments. Becoming a nuisance to one's broker is not the way to develop a good working relationship.

If you are inexperienced in the stock market or are unsure of your tolerance for risk, select low-risk transactions.

A Final Note

After finding a competent, ethical broker, treat him or her with consideration, loyalty, and respect. Brokers as a group are subjected to criticism for any poor advice they give. On the other hand, they hear little praise for suggestions which work out well. Showing your appreciation for good performance could make you a favorite customer. Some words of thanks for the winners might motivate the broker to work harder for you.

Postscript

It's not an easy task to control your emotions as the stock market moves through its cycle and others surrender to greed, euphoria, or panic. The exercises in this book give you the opportunity to review the relative strength of your own feelings. Acknowledging your emotional inclinations is the first step toward learning to control them.

I've provided a framework for developing control over your emotions and presented suggestions for dealing with them when they arise. I've offered three long-term strategies which can help you avoid the emotional reactions that accompany the short-term fluctuations of the market. I've outlined a program of self-education to eliminate dependence on a stock broker which can lead to problems.

The stock market provides an atmosphere in which emotions can get out of control. Those who surrender to this crowd psychology buy when others are eager to buy, and sell when others are selling in panic. This is a losing approach because it results in buying at high prices and selling at low prices. Those who learn to control their emotions buy when prices are low at market bottoms, and sell when prices are high at market tops. After you develop the ability to control your emotions so you can follow this rational approach, you will be better able to beat the market in the years to come.

Appendix A

References and Information Sources

The following listing of references and information sources is presented to help you in your program of self-education. Many of these references are available in public libraries.

1. Basic Information

Downes, John and Jordan Goodman. *Barron's Finance and Investment Handbook.* Woodbury, New York: John Barron's Educational Services, Inc., 1986.

This book contains information on how to read annual and quarterly reports, the stock quotes in the newspapers, and the ticker tape. It also gives definitions of 2500 investment terms and investment vehicles such as common stock, preferred stock, convertible preferred stock, etc.

Engle, Louis, *How to Buy Stocks.* New York: Little, Brown & Co., 1990.

Investor's Rights Manual. New York: New York Institute of Finance, 1989.

This manual outlines an investor's rights and responsibilities and the regulations designed to protect him or her from illegal practices. Legal recourses available when an investor has been mistreated are also described.

Littauer, Stephen. *How to Buy Mutual Funds.* Palm City, FL: Montebello Press, 1989.

Scott, David L. *How Wall Street Works,* Chicago: Probus, 1992.

Standard and Poor's Stock Guide. New York: Standard and Poor Corp. Updated and revised each month.

This booklet provides basic financial data on over 5,000 common and preferred stocks. It also gives statistics on several hundred mutual funds of all types. Your broker will probably have past issues which you may borrow.

Standard and Poor's Stock Reports. New York: Standard and Poor Corp. Updated and revised each quarter.

These reports—each consisting of a single sheet—provide an overview of a company's operations, a review of recent corporate developments, information on past earnings, and prospects for future earnings. Copies of these reports are available for reference in many brokerage offices and libraries.

Value Line Investment Survey Reports. New York: Value Line Investment Survey Corporation. Published weekly.

These reports—each consisting of a single page—provide an overview of company operations and earnings prospects. The reports rate each company's stock for timeliness of purchase, safety and volatility. The 100 stocks with the lowest price to earnings ratios are also identified. Included in the report is a chart showing a fifteen-year history of the stock price fluctuations along with an estimate of the price appreciation in the next three to five years.

An important feature of this service is that it allows comparison of each company with others in the same industry. *Value Line Investment Survey* is available in some brokers' offices,

libraries, and from Value Line Investment Survey at 711 Third Ave., New York, NY 10017.

Wall Street Week. PBS.

This weekly television program is presented Friday nights by your Public Broadcasting System station. It provides a review of the week's activities on the stock market, predictions of market direction, and an interview with a specialist in a selected industry. Check your local television listing for broadcast time in your area.

2. Stock Selection Techniques

The references listed below can help you learn how to select Stocks that will help your portfolio increase faster than the market averages and indices.

Form 10K

The Securities Exchange Commission requires the annual completion and submission of these reports from each company listed on the stock exchanges. These forms give detailed information on the nature of each corporation's business, management, competition, outstanding debt, and other factors that affect a company's operations and prospects. These forms can also be obtained without charge from many companies.

Hardy, Colburn. *Blue Chip Investment Strategy.* New York: Franklin Watts, 1987.

This book outlines a method for evaluating blue chip stocks to select those that are best positioned for achieving capital gains.

Lynch, Peter. *One Up on Wall Street.* New York: Simon & Schuster, 1989.

This book tells the reader how to identify promising invest-ments from observations of new, successful products in the stores. It also provides tips for analyzing company financial sta-tus to find those that are undervalued by the market.

Richie, John Jr. *Fundamental Analysis*. Chicago: Probus, 1991.

This book provides basic information on how to analyze the financial condition of companies for the purpose of selecting high-quality investments.

Woelfel, Charles. *Financial Statement Analysis*. Chicago: Probus, 1991.

This book outlines the procedures for analyzing quarterly and annual financial reports.

3. Timing the Market Cycle

The references listed here can assist you in timing the tops and bottoms of market cycles. The ability to recognize a market top as an opportunity to sell at high prices and a market bottom as a chance to buy at low prices is important to your success in using Strategy #2 of #3.

Link, Albert. *Mastering the Business Cycle*. Chicago: Probus, 1991.

Stoken, Dick. *Strategic Investment Timing in the '90s*. Chicago: Probus, 1991.

4. Staying Informed

Cable News Network (CNN)
This cable television station broadcasts a stock market report called "Business Day" in the mornings and "Moneyline" in the

evenings, Monday through Friday. Consult your local television listing for program broadcast times in your area.

Consumer & Financial News Network (CNBC/FNN).
This cable television station provides current reports on the stock market, individual companies, and other financial matters. It displays ticker tapes of stock prices traded on the N.Y. Stock Exchange and on the over-the-counter market with a broadcast time delay of 15 minutes.

Investor's Business Daily.
A national newspaper which provides authoritative reports on economic, industry and company events.

Wall Street Journal.
This nationally distributed newspaper provides authoritative daily reports on economic, industry, and company events.

5. Psychology and the Market

Galbraith, Kenneth. *A Short History of Financial Euphoria.* Knoxville, Tenn: Whittle Communications L.P., 1990.
This book analyzes the psychology of the speculative factors involved in the mass financial euphorias of present and past generations. It demonstrates how the common factors of excessive greed and speculation underlie each of these financial disasters.

Mehrabian, Albert. *Your Inner Path to Investment Success.* Chicago: Probus, 1991.
This book outlines eight different types of investor temperaments and helps the reader identify his or her own. The author shows the investor how to fine tune his or her investment style to maximize profits.

Tuccile, Jerome. *Mind over Money.* New York: William Morrow & Co., 1980.

This book explains how some investors let greed, guilt, and fear interfere with their chances for success in the market. The author alerts the reader to the avaricious broker, and provides guidelines for developing a sound approach to investing in the stock market.

6. Commercial Stock Chart Publishers

Listed below are several services which publish up-to-date charts of companies listed on the stock exchanges.

Daily Graphs. P.O. Box 24933, Los Angeles, CA 90024.

Mansfield Stock Charts. 2973 Kennedy Blvd., Jersey City, NJ 07306.

Securities Research Corp. 208 Newbury St., Boston, MA 02116.

Trendline, Inc. 25 Broadway, New York, NY 10004.

Before selecting any of these chart services, you may wish to visit your public library. If they are available there, you'll have the opportunity to see which best suits your needs.

Appendix B

 # Glossary

ACCOUNT CHURNING—Excessive trading in a customer's account for the primary purpose of generating commissions for the broker.

ADVISORY LETTER—A publication containing advice for investors. These letters are published periodically by individuals or companies, and are distributed to their subscribers. The letters advise buying, selling. or holding specific investments.

AMERICAN STOCK EXCHANGE—This exchange lists medium- and small-sized companies. Its standard for listing a company is lower than that of the New York Stock Exchange, and the volume of stocks traded is much smaller. Address: 86 Trinity Place, New York, NY 10006.

ASCENDING TRIANGLE—A stock price pattern characterized by two or more tops at approximately the same level, and two or more bottoms with each successive bottom being higher than the preceding bottom. An ascending line drawn across the bottoms intersects with the horizontal line drawn across the tops. (The third side of the triangle is not drawn because it does not define the boundaries of the price fluctuation.) The upward slant of the bottom line reflects the increasing demand as compared to the supply (see 6–13 for an example.)

BEAR MARKET—A period of time during which stock averages trend downward and any upward price movements are relatively short in distance and duration.

BLIND POOL—A sum of money assembled for speculation in an unspecified enterprise or enterprises. After the money has been collected by the pool organizers, they determine which venture or ventures to finance. This type of venture financing is extremely risky because the failure rate among new companies is very high.

BLUE CHIP—A financially strong, well-known company with good management which has demonstrated its ability to maintain its dividend through bull and bear markets.

BOILER ROOM—This phrase refers to stock selling operations in which high pressure is used to sell shares to the general public. Stock salespersons use telephones to contact prospects and sell them penny stocks and other speculative stock issues. Some of these boiler room operations sell fraudulent securities.

BOTTOM OUT—This phrase refers to the conversion of a bear market into a bull market as demand begins to exceed supply. The phrase may also refer to the performance of individual stocks. Note that some stocks bottom out before the market, some bottom out with the market, and some bottom out afterwards.

BULL MARKET—A period of time during which stock averages trend upward and any downward price movements are relatively short in distance and duration.

CALL OPTION—The right to buy a specified number of shares of a company's stock at a stated price until a specified date in the future. An individual who buys a call option believes the price of the stock will rise enough to cover the purchase cost and provide for a profit. If the price of the stock does not rise, or goes down, and the buyer does not sell or exercise the option before the expiration date, it becomes worthless.

CAPITAL GAIN—The amount of profit made on a transaction. If the price of the stock goes up after it is purchased, and it is then sold, the sale price will be higher than the purchase price. This difference, after subtracting the cost of the transaction, is the capital gain.

CAPITAL LOSS—The amount of loss suffered in a transaction. If the price goes down after the stock is purchased, and it is then sold, the selling price will be lower than the purchase price. The difference, after adding in the cost of the transaction, is the capital loss.

CEO—See Chief Executive Officer.

CHAPTER 11 OF BANKRUPTCY CODE—The chapter of the Bankruptcy Code which allows the declarer of bankruptcy to continue business operations under protection of the law from its creditors, such as suppliers and bond holders.

CHIEF EXECUTIVE OFFICER (CEO)—The top operating officer in a corporation. He or she exercises command over all corporate activities.

COMMON STOCK—A certificate representing ownership in a corporation which entitles the holder to voting rights and a proportionate share of dividends declared on the stock.

CONTRARIAN—One who takes the opposite point of view to that held by an overwhelming majority. This viewpoint is most appropriate during euphoric buying and panic selling conditions.

COVERED SHORT SALE—This is a short sale in which the seller holds a number of shares equal to or greater than those sold.

CYCLICAL INDUSTRY—An industry whose profits rise and fall with the economic cycle. When the economy is doing well, the companies in a cyclical industry prosper. When the economy does poorly, the profits made by the companies in the industry decline or may disappear.

DEBT TO EQUITY RATIO—This ratio is obtained by dividing the dollar amount of long-term debt by the stockholders' equity in the company. For example if the long-term debt is $1,000,000 and the stockholders' equity is $5,000,000, the debt to equity ratios is .20 or 20 percent. Companies with high ratios are in greater danger of going bankrupt than companies with low ratios because a company with a large amount of debt may not be able to pay the interest on the loan when income declines.

DELAYED OPENING—A late start in the trading of the shares of a company. The delay is ordered because of a large imbalance in the amount of stock for sale and the amount desired for purchase. The delay gives the specialist or the market maker time to assess the situation and determine how far to raise or lower the price to reduce the imbalance. (Raising the price can induce more holders to sell. Lowering the price can induce more investors to buy.)

DEMAND—The volume of shares of a company's stock sought for purchase by buyers. The amount of this volume changes continually. When the amount of shares sought for purchase at a particular price is greater than the number of shares available for sale at that price, the price is forced upward.

DESCENDING TRIANGLE—A stock price pattern characterized by two or more bottoms at approximately the same level, and two or more tops with each successive top being lower than the preceding top. A straight line drawn across the bottoms will intersect with the descending line drawn across the tops. (The third side of the triangle is not drawn because it does not serve to define the boundaries of the price fluctuation.) The downward slant reflects increasing supply as compared to demand (see Figure 6–6 for an example.)

DISCOUNT BROKER—A discount broker charges less commission to execute a transaction than a full service broker. Discount brokers keep their costs and commissions lower by not providing advice or research reports to their clients. Individuals who know what transactions they want to make can use a discount broker to save a major portion of the commission.

DISCRETIONARY ACCOUNT—A discretionary account agreement, when signed by the customer, authorizes the broker to make transactions in the account without the prior approval or the knowledge of the client. The broker is therefore able to buy and sell at her or his own discretion.

DISCRETIONARY FUNDS—The amount available for investment after budgeted needs such as food, clothing, shelter, transportation costs, insurance, etc. have been taken into account.

DIVERSIFICATION—The concept of investing in a large number of industries to reduce the risk by spreading it around. This increases the safety of the invested capital. A person with a large amount of capital can diversify his or her own investments. An individual with a small amount of capital can make a diversified investment by buying shares in a mutual fund which owns stocks in many different segments of the economy.

DOWNTREND LINE—A line drawn through two or more descending tops. The downtrend remains in effect until the price penetrates to the other side of the line (see Figure 6–1 for an example.)

DOUBLE BOTTOM—The pattern formed when the price of a stock which has made one bottom declines again to the same approximate level, makes a second bottom, and then rises once again (see Figure 6–10 for an example.)

DOUBLE TOP—The pattern formed when the price of a stock which has peaked once rises again to the same approximate level, makes a second top, and then declines again (see Figure 6–3 for an example.)

EQUITY FUND—A mutual fund which invests only in instruments of ownership such as common stock or preferred stock.

FORTUNE 500 COMPANY—Each year *Fortune* magazine lists and ranks the 500 largest industrial corporations. A company appearing in this list is called a Fortune 500 company.

FREE FALL—The rapid decline in the price of a stock or a stock average when there is little or no hesitation in the descent. The free fall continues as long as the sellers are much more anxious to sell than the buyers are to buy.

FULL SERVICE BROKER—A full service firm does not discount its commissions to attract customers. Instead it offers additional services above those offered by discount brokers, for example, research reports, investment advice, and information about specific companies on request.

GROWTH COMPANY—A company which manufactures a product or products, or provides a service or services for which the demand is greater than the supply. These companies usually enjoy a pattern of strong earnings growth until supply catches up with demand.

GROWTH INDUSTRY—An industry which supplies products or services for which the demand is far greater than the supply. A growth industry usually enjoys relatively large profit margins.

GROWTH STOCK FUND—A mutual fund which specializes in growth companies selected from growth industries. The objective of a growth stock fund is to achieve large capital gains.

HEAD AND SHOULDERS—This pattern is formed when the price of a stock rise to a peak, declines, then rises to a higher peak, declines again, and then rises to a third peak lower than the second. The first and third peaks are usually about the same height. This sequence of prices gives the rough appearance of a crude head and shoulders (see Figure 6–2 for an example.)

HEDGING ACTION—This is an action which limits risk and protects against loss. This is done by making counter balancing transactions in which the two positions move in opposite directions. When one goes up, the other goes down, and vice versa.

For example, in December an investor might have a large capital gain which, because of tax considerations, she does not want to take until January. To protect herself against a decline in the stock before she sells, she could buy a put option on that stock. Then, if the price of the stock went down, the decline would be covered by her gain from the sale of the put option. If the price of the stock went up, her loss from the put option would be offset by her additional gain in the stock.

HOT TIP—This is unofficial information about a company, passed along by word of mouth and supposedly not yet known by the public. The information passed along in this matter is often inaccurate and sometimes completely untrue. It is a poor basis on which to make an investment decision.

INDEX FUND—This type of fund is designed to track a major stock index. The purpose of this approach is to be certain the performance of this fund will approximate the performance of the tracked index over the long term.

INITIAL PUBLIC OFFERING (IPO)—This is the original offering of shares in a company which is going public. The money raised in this fashion can be used to start up a new company or to expand one that is already in business. Some of the companies which issue stock for purchase by the general public are sound, profitable businesses. However, many IPOs are the means for financing companies which are in the research and development phase. These companies may be run by management which is inexperienced at marketing a product or service and which has not shown its ability to earn a profit.

INSIDE TRADING—An inside trade is one made prior to the public release of material information capable of moving the price of the company's stock up or down significantly. Securities and Exchange Commission regulations prohibit inside trading and prescribe fines and jail sentences for violation of these regulations.

LEVERAGE—The extra buying power achieved by borrowing money to increase the size of a purchase (see MARGIN ACCOUNT.)

LIQUID ASSETS—Cash or other assets that can be easily and quickly converted into cash.

LONG TERM—This phrase refers to a period of at least one year, but usually much longer.

MARGIN ACCOUNT—An account which allows an individual to borrow a portion of the price of the transaction from the broker. The loan enables a customer to purchase additional shares above and beyond those for which he has cash. The leverage from this extra buying power increases the potential both for profits and losses.

MARGIN CALL—A demand by the broker for more money or collateral from the customer. The broker makes the margin call when she decides the value of the account has declined to the danger point with regard to the customer's ability to repay the loan from the equity in the account. The customer can respond to the margin call by depositing more cash or collateral in the account, or by selling shares of stock to raise the required amount of cash.

MARKET MAKER—A dealer who coordinates transactions in particular stocks outside of the regular auction markets conducted by the established stock exchanges. The market maker receives both buy and sell orders from brokers acting on behalf of their customers. When the buy orders outnumber the sell orders, the dealer raises the price or sells from his own account. When sell orders outnumber buy orders, the dealer lowers the price or buys for his own account. The dealer maintains a spread between the bid price to buy and the offer price to sell. The dealer keeps this difference as compensation for making the transaction.

MARKET ORDER—An order to sell or buy at the current price— whatever it is. A person putting in an order to buy a stock "at the market," pays the price of the lowest current offer to sell. A person putting in an order to sell "at the market," receives the highest current bid price.

MARKET SHARE—The percentage of the total market sales volume made by each company in that industry. For example, the total U.S. sales of cars and trucks are divided up among the American and foreign vehicle manufacturers. Each manufacturer has a measurable percentage of the total sales in the U.S. This figure is that manufacturer's market share.

NASDAQ—See National Association of Securities Dealers Automated Quote system.

NATIONAL ASSOCIATION OF SECURITIES DEALERS AUTOMATED QUOTE SYSTEM—This is a nationwide electronic network of automated stock quotation display devices. It provides up-to-the-minute price quotes of stocks which are not listed on the stock exchanges.

NEW ISSUE—Additional shares being offered by the company. These shares can be offered to the general public or they can be placed privately. The cash raised in this manner can be used to expand operations, retire debt, finance purchases of other companies, etc.

NEW YORK STOCK EXCHANGE—This is the largest exchange in the United States. It lists the largest, most well known companies, and many smaller ones. It has the highest standard for listing companies. Address: 11 Wall Street, New York, NY 10005

OUT OF THE MONEY OPTION—This phrase is used in reference to put and call options. A call option is out of the money when the market price of the stock is below the price at which the call option holder may buy the stock.

For example, if a call option authorizes its holder to buy ABC Corporation at $10.00 per share, and ABC stock is currently trading at $9.00 per share, there would be no profit in exercising the call option, so it is said to be "out of the money."

A put option is out of the money when the market price of the stock is above the price at which the put option authorizes its holder to sell the stock. Thus, if a put option authorizes its holder to sell the stock at $9.00 a share, and the stock is currently trading at $10.00 a share, the put option would be "out of the money."

OVERBOUGHT—The excessively high price which occurs after a period of euphoric buying. The price becomes susceptible to a precipitous fall because of its unjustified rise.

OVERSOLD—The excessively low price which occurs after a period of panic selling. The price becomes susceptible to a sharp rise because of the unjustified decline.

PANIC SELLING—An exceptionally large volume of selling (supply of stock) which overwhelms the buyers' demand for stock. The result of this temporary imbalance is a free fall in prices. When panic selling occurs at the bottom of a bear market, it is called a selling climax.

PAPER LOSS—An unmaterialized loss. The difference between the price paid and the price that would be obtained if the stock were sold after a decline.

PAPER PROFIT—An unmaterialized profit. The difference between the price paid and the price that would be obtained if the stock were sold after a rise.

PENNY STOCK—The Securities and Exchange Commission definition is a stock that trades over the counter and sells for less than five dollars a share. The term can also be applied to any stock which sells for less than one dollar a share no matter where it trades.

PINK SHEETS—These sheets list companies which do not qualify for any stock exchange and are not included in the National Association of Securities Dealers Automated Quotation system (NASDAQ). A few dealers make a market in these stocks. Bid and asked spreads are usually large. The buyer has a sizable paper loss immediately after purchase.

PRICE/EARNINGS RATIO—This ratio is obtained by dividing the market price of the stock by the earnings for the year. If the price of the stock is $10. per share, and the company earned $1. per share, the price/earnings ratio is ten to one.

PROFIT MARGIN—This is the ratio of gross profits to net sales, which can be expressed as a percentage. For example, if gross profits are ten million dollars, and net sales are one hundred million, the profit margin is 10 percent.

PUT OPTION—The right to sell a specified number of shares of a company's stock at a stated price until a specific date in the future. An individual who buys a put option believes the price of the stock will fall enough to cover the purchase cost and to provide a profit. If the price does not fall, or rises, and the buyer does not sell or exercise the option before the expiration date, it becomes worthless at that time.

REPORT OF INSIDER TRADING—This report, which is available from the United States Printing Office, shows the trades by corporate officials in their own companies. These trades must be reported to the Securities and Exchange Commission within the first ten days of the month following the month in which the trade was made.

RESISTANCE LEVEL—This phrase refers to the highest price in a price pattern whose top boundary line is horizontal (see Figure 6–13 for an example.)

RIGHTS TO PURCHASE STOCK—This is a privilege given to current shareholders to buy additional shares at a price below the market price. Some shareholders who do not wish to buy additional shares sell their rights on the market.

Rights have a life span of a few weeks. Anyone who buys these rights on the market must either resell them or exercise them by putting up the required cash to buy the appropriate number of shares before noon on the expiration date, when they become worthless.

ROUNDING BOTTOM—The saucer shaped curve which develops when a downtrend in a stock price gradually changes into an uptrend over a period of several months or longer (see Figure 6–12 for an example.)

ROUNDING TOP—The upside down saucer shaped curve which develops when an uptrend in a stock price gradually changes into a downtrend over a period of several months or longer (see Figure 6–5 for an example.)

RUMOR—A favorable or unfavorable story about a company which has not been released officially by that company. Rumors are usually passed from person to person, although they may also be reported in the media.

SECURITIES EXCHANGE COMMISSION (SEC)—This is the government agency responsible for the regulation and oversight of securities trading and the enforcement of securities laws.

SECTOR FUND—A fund which specializes in companies in the same industry or sector of the economy. For example, a sector fund might specialize in utility companies, the health care industry, telecommunications, medical research, banks, precious metals, natural resources, chemicals, electronics, energy, leisure, real estate, biotechnology, etc.

SELLING CLIMAX—An event where prices go into a free fall, trading volume expands to record levels, prices hit bottom ,and within a day or two start rising rapidly. This dramatic event occurs at the bottom of some bear markets and signals the start of the new bull market.

SELLING SHORT—The sale of shares that have been borrowed. The seller must eventually repurchase the shares and return them to the lender. If the price of the stock declines after the sale, the seller can repurchase the stock at the lower price. The difference in price, minus the cost of the transaction, is the profit. If the price rises after the sale, the short seller must buy the shares back at the higher price. The loss is the difference in price plus the costs of the transactions.

SHORTING AGAINST THE BOX—This is a hedging action to limit a loss or protect a profit. See COVERED SHORT SALE.

SHORT TERM—This phrase refers to a period of time up to a few months.

SPECIALIST—A member of the stock exchange who works on the floor of the exchange and is responsible for maintaining an orderly market in one or more stocks. To do this she may have to buy or sell for her own account to counterbalance a temporary excess of supply or demand.

STOCK PURCHASE RIGHTS—See RIGHTS TO PURCHASE STOCK.

STOP ORDER—An order to buy or sell a stock when the price reaches a specified level.

STOP LOSS ORDER—An order to sell a stock if it declines to a specified level. It would then become an order to sell at the market. This type of sell order is used to protect a profit or limit a loss.

STRAIGHT LINE PROJECTION—The tendency of stock market analysts to predict that a market which has been rising a long time will continue to rise.

SUPPLY—The volume of a company's shares available for sale. The amount of this volume varies continually. When the supply of shares available at a particular price is greater than the demand for shares at that price, the price is forced lower.

SUPPORT LEVEL—This phrase refers to the lowest price in a price pattern whose lower boundary line is horizontal (see Figure 6–6 for an example.)

TOPPING OUT—This phrase refers to the conversion of a bull market into a bear market as supply begins to exceed demand. The phrase may also refer to the performance of individual stocks. Note that some stocks top out before the market, some top out with the market, and some top out after it.

TRADING VOLUME—The trading volume is the number of shares traded in the course of a day, week, month, or year. These figures are published in many newspapers.

TRIPLE BOTTOM—This pattern is formed when the price of a stock which has made a double bottom declines again to the approximate level of the two preceding bottoms, and then rises again (see Figure 6–11 for an example.)

TRIPLE TOP—This pattern is formed when the price of a stock which has made a double top rises again to the approximate level of the two preceding tops, and then falls again (see Figure 6–4 for an example.)

UNCOVERED SHORT SALE—This phrase refers to selling a quantity of shares short without owning an equal number of shares in the same company. The customer borrows the shares from a lender and sells them on the market. Her hope is to buy the shares back at a lower price and return them to the lender. Her profit from this transaction would be the difference between the price at which she sold short and the price at which she purchased the shares back—minus the cost of the transaction. However, if the price goes up, there's no limit on how much she can lose because there's no limit to how high the price might go.

UNDERWRITER—An investment banker or a syndicate which agrees to cooperate with an issuer of stock by purchasing the stock and distributing it. The underwriter buys the stock at a price that is lower than the price at which it is offered to the public.

UPTREND LINE—A line drawn through two or more ascending bottoms. The uptrend remains in effect until the price penetrates to the other side of the line (see Figure 6–2 for an example.)

VENTURE CAPITAL—This is capital raised to help a new business get started. Companies which seek venture capital have usually been unsuccessful in obtaining financing from the standard sources of capital such as banks, insurance companies, or other credit oriented institutions. Since most of these new companies are unproven in the marketplace, the risks associated with providing venture capital are high.

WARRANT TO PURCHASE—This is the right to buy a stock at a price above the current market price. This right usually extends for several years, but some warrants are perpetual. Warrants are traded on the open market. Warrants which have an expiration date become worthless on that date.

WHISTLE BLOWER—A company employee with a strong conscience. If such an employee is aware of unethical or illegal activities within a company and reports it to proper authorities in the government, he or she is referred to as a whistle blower.

ZERO SUM GAME—An investment transaction in which the two participants take opposite points of view. One party believes the price will rise, and the other party believes it will fall. The one who is right makes a profit which is equal to the loss suffered by the one who was wrong. The sum of the profit, which is a positive figure, when added to the loss, which is a negative figure, equals zero.

Bibliography

Burgauer, James. *The Do-It-Yourself-Investor.* Chicago: Probus Publishing, 1987.

Cardiff, Gray. *Panic Proof Investing.* New York: Prentiss Hall, 1988.

Galbraith, John Kenneth. *A Short History of Financial Euphoria. Knoxville, Tennessee: Whittle Communications, 1990.*

Gitman, Lawrence, and Michael Joehnk. *Investment Fundamentals.* New York: Harper & Row, 1899.

Gurney, Kathleen. *Your Money Personality.* New York: Doubleday, 1988.

Hardy, C. Colburn. *Blue Chip Investment Strategy.* New York: Franklin Watts, 1987.

Lynch, Peter. *One Up On Wall Street.* New York: Simon and Schuster, 1989.

Mehrabian, Albert. *Your Inner Path to Investment Success.* Chicago: Probus Publishing, 1991.

Pistolese, Clifford. *Using Technical Analysis.* Chicago: Probus Publishing, 1989.

Rolo, Charles, and Robert Klein. *Gaining on the Market*. Boston: Little, Brown & Co., 1988.

Schultz, Harry. *Panics and Crashes*. Westport, Connecticut: Arlington House, 1980.

Tuccile, Jerome. *Mind Over Money*. New York: William Morrow & Co., 1980.

Index

About the Publisher

PROBUS PUBLISHING COMPANY

Probus Publishing Company fills the informational needs of today's business professional by publishing authoritative, quality books on timely and relevant topics, including:

- Investing
- Futures/Options Trading
- Banking
- Finance
- Marketing and Sales
- Manufacturing and Project Management
- Personal Finance, Real Estate, Insurance and Estate Planning
- Entrepreneurship
- Management

Probus books are available at quantity discounts when purchased for business, educational or sales promotional use. For more information, please call the Director, Corporate/Institutional Sales at 1-800-PROBUS-1, or write:

Director, Corporate/Institutional Sales
Probus Publishing Company
1925 N. Clybourn Avenue
Chicago, Illinois 60614
FAX (312) 868-6250